# REVAMP
## Pathway To Recovery

# REVAMP
## Pathway To Recovery

by
## Lance Johnson

# Table of Contents

# FORWORD

I do not believe anyone sets out in life to become a notorious sinner. By that I mean, no one wakes up one day and decides I want to be an alcoholic or a drug addict. Then spend countless days in jail and pay enormous fines for driving drunk. Eventually lose custody of children, destroy the trust and respect of the ones who love them most and see their hopes and dreams destroyed. Even though one does not set out with these goals, it happens to countless people every day. No matter who they may be or where they come from, it happens because ultimately sin has set its sights on all. Sin is not prejudice. It does not care if a person is black or white, yellow or red, male or female, rich or poor, educated or uneducated, what country they are from or who their family is. Sin simply seeks all and wants to appear to be the best thing that ever happened to a person.

This is my story of how sin sought me out and became the destroyer of my life. My life is much like that of the prodigal son told about in Luke 15:11-32. I thought there was a great life away from God and I was determined to live life to its fullest. Like the prodigal son, I ended up in the pig pen.

I grew up in what is considered by most to be an average American Christian home. I grew up in a very well structured family atmosphere. My mother and father were both good parents and providers. I could say I had the best of childhoods. Even though I grew up in a good home where we went to church occasionally and I claimed to be a Christian. I still chose to take a very destructive road that would lead to disaster.

I remember my first encounter with alcohol. I was in the 8th grade around the age of 12 when some of my friends and I decided to go to one of their parent's homes and raid the hidden liquor cabinet. It was certainly not the taste of the alcohol that tempted us or even the feeling it gave us. I think it was simply the curiosity and feeling of being grown and macho that got us. Sin disguises itself in many deceptive forms, it does not care how or why you chose it. It only desires for you to yield to its temptation. Even though we all became staggering drunk, we did not become alcoholics over this one event. My second experience with substances came from marijuana just a short time after, it also came as a result of curiosity. Even though I never cared for the taste of alcohol or the high of smoking marijuana, I would eventually yield to the temptation as a way of life. These were only opportunities for me to familiarize with the sins that would eventually control my life and take me places I wish I'd never gone. Sin never reveals its agenda. In the beginning it simply starts out by appearing fun and harmless, but as you continue to dance with it, the agenda will certainly manifest in a big way. By high school, it became the need to fit in and be accepted among my peers that would cause me to use alcohol and drugs on a regular basis. The thing that must be understood about sin is it can have a variety of methods for tempting a person. To some, alcohol and drugs are a way of dealing with life's problems, To others, illicit sex can become a way in which a rejected person can feel accepted and loved. As a former founder and president of a large drug and alcohol facility, I meet people who turn to drugs as a result to childhood abuse, failed marriages, bankruptcy and many more. You name it and I have heard it, how sin can enter into a person's life. Sin has a way of making us think it is just what we need. Whether it's the comfort alcohol gives a person who is hurting, or the feeling un-forgiveness and anger gives a person who has been done wrong. Lying is also a sin and can make a person feel better about themselves if they are not happy with who they are. What most people might be afraid to say is that sin no matter what kind like; sex, drunkenness, lying, stealing, envy or jealousy. Sin feels good and has what appears to be some benefits and rewards.

Because sin had some really good benefits, so I thought, I jumped in head first. Alcohol and sex became the way to high school popularity. Eventually drugs would become a method of fulfilling my aspirations of becoming a successful football player. What I did not realize was the control it had over my life. During my sophomore and junior year of high school I do not remember going to school without first going to the bootlegger's house and buying a half pint of bourbon whiskey. The bootlegger's house was only a few minutes from my high school, and I would down the whole bottle before I arrived at school. By noon, the high would wear off and I did this almost every day. On top of that I would party and drink almost every weekend. All of this was so I could fit in and be in the click, or at least so I thought. The amazing thing about all this, is I was able to hide it from everyone except those I wanted to know. It was not that my parents and teachers were naïve, it was the fact that with the sin came a power of manipulation and craftiness. What many fail to realize is that Satan is the instigator of sin. When we accept his temptations we take on his nature. Sin wants you to succeed in allowing yourself to continue under its power, and Satan will give you the ability to do just that, at least for a little while. My entire high school experience seemed to be what most teens would desire. I achieved, in my mind, all my goals from popularity to having the hottest girlfriends and even my goal of being an outstanding football player. I received a full scholarship to Jacksonville State University based on my football abilities. I was able to accomplish all this while living in complete sin. I must say sin will give you a season of satisfaction. This why one will continue in sin and pursue it with such passion. I must warn you, it only last for a season. I will talk more about the cost of sin in a later chapter.

I graduated high school and continued to pursue my goals while drinking and drugs remained a part of my lifestyle. I eventually left my scholarship and education for what was at that time, the love of my life. A short time after leaving college I purchased a home and married all in an effort to find happiness. After a year of marriage I ended up going through a bitter divorce, mostly due to the effect the drugs and alcohol had on my life. At the time, I did not realize the sin that had a grip on my life was costing me the things I loved the most. After the divorce, the use of drugs and alcohol became much more frequent than anytime in the past. It became a way to deal with the pain of the divorce, and an instrument in allowing me to achieve some sort of social and peer acceptance. Because I was the big party guy and always had drugs, friends were never scarce. Being surrounded by people who appeared to enjoy my company became a way of dealing with the rejection and failure I felt from my divorce, it gave me a sense of worth. Sex became a way of gaining self esteem that would soon prove to be self-deception, fueled by a monstrous ego and unbridled pride. To my shame, I confess I had turned into a pride driven jerk with no respect for myself or anyone else. Because of this I left behind me a trail of broken relationships, but in my eyes I was "the man" and living the ultimate life. All the problems and conflict in my life was in my eyes, someone else's fault. I had the ability to manipulate circumstances and situations so I could twist everything around to point the blame on anyone but myself. The need for success and material gain became another controlling factor in my life that would become as deadly and enslaving as the drug and alcohol addiction. I was absolutely driven by the need for drugs, wealth, and sex. In that arena, I seemed to have it all a home in a country club, a new car every few months, and a different woman each night. The more money I had the more power it gave me to have drugs, seduce and entice women, and make them think that I could give them whatever they wanted. I lived almost every night in strip clubs seducing and exploiting women with my so called charm, wealth, and power. Although I was surrounded by relationships of every kind there was an empty void in my life that I was desperately seeking to fill. The more I got, the more I wanted. I was just like the prodigal son traveling down a road of my own creation doing things my way, but as empty and lonely as a person could be.

I eventually married my wife Lisa in an effort to find that satisfaction I was so desperately seeking after. Even though our love for each other was genuine, it was still not enough. After a year of marriage, we planned for a family and found out we would be blessed with our daughter Brittany. The birth of my daughter was one of those significant moments that would change most people's life forever, but in my case the change did not last. As much as I loved my daughter I continued to live the same destructive lifestyle. For many people the birth of a child or a solid relationship might change their life, but in my case nothing was strong enough to break the hold that sin had on my life. There would be countless nights my wife and daughter would sleep alone wondering where daddy was and would he ever come home? To me I was doing nothing wrong, I was just living my dream. Most people underestimate the power sin can have over one's life. I have watched as mothers have abandoned their responsibilities to their children to the point they lose custody of them due to their addiction. I have watched as husbands and wives have destroyed stable homes and jeopardized the future of their children for the pleasure of an affair. The controlling power of sin can cause a son or daughter to steal from their parents until they have taken their financial security and left the parents with nothing. It has caused people to go in and out of the judicial system, spending months and years in prison, paying countless thousands of dollars in fines, all due to sin they can't give up. Most people find this type of behavior hard to comprehend, but it is the power sin can have over a person's life.

Because of the sin in my life and the change it had brought, I found myself separating from my family and friends. While developing new friendships that embraced my way of life. Sin is an enemy that desires to isolate and separate you from those who have a positive influence upon your life. Sin is like the Philistine giant "Goliath", the enemy that came against the army of Israel. He always wanted to fight just one of the men from the army of Israel because the chances were he could defeat any ONE, but not the whole army. The strange thing about this, is that while I was separating myself from my family and friends who had a positive influence on my life. I thought of them as my enemies because they stood in the way of me getting what I wanted, when in fact they were trying to save my life. Looking back, I can clearly see how the enemy worked and I pray others may also see how the enemy of sin is working to destroy anything and everything that is good in their life. As a Pastor, I watch young people make their parents their enemies all due to the fact they are trying to be a positive influence on their lives, but they want something else. When sin has its way, it will make God your enemy because He is ultimately the one who wants to influence you in what is right, but to have your way you must attempt in separating yourself from God. I made the church my enemy by using excuses like, "the church is full of hypocrites and judgmental people". I eventually made God my enemy by holding Him responsible for a tragic event that occurred in my life. When I was just 10 years old my Grandfather, who was a very significant part of my life, committed suicide during a nervous breakdown. During that breakdown he blamed me for his condition, and a few hours later shot himself in my presence. As I grew older I blamed God for this and held Him responsible for this terrible tragedy. In fact, God was not responsible for what happened that day. The things that happened, and the words that were spoken were the results of the nervous breakdown he experienced. For me it was my excuse to reject God and refuse to yield to His love and calling on my life. It never ceases to amaze me how

xi

we can hold God responsible for things that happen in our lives that He had nothing to do with, some things we brought on ourselves. This is truly the deception of Satan, these are the crafty devices he uses to remove us from anyone who has the power to help us. I had become just like the prodigal son. By the fact that I had joined myself to a citizen of a foreign country as far away from God and family as I could get.

The friends and relationships I developed helped empower me to obtain the sinful things I desired most. They encouraged me, they gave to me, they covered up for me, and they even bonded me out of jail when necessary. Choosing wrong relationships is definitely a way to strengthen your ability to get what you want. They will certainly help you in achieving your desires, but where they send you, you may not want to go. Just like the citizen of a foreign country sent the prodigal son to the pig pen, wrong relationships will send you to the bottom. One of the greatest revelations I have ever received from the word of God came from John 15 verses 5-6. It compares us to a vine and its branches with Jesus being the vine and us being the branches. If we choose not to abide in Him, we will be cut off and cast aside where we will wither or become weak and men, not Satan, will gather us up and cast us into the fire. When we choose to separate ourselves from God, men will then have the influence and control to determine our destinies and will most certainly be a destructive one. The friends I chose only empowered me for the destructive crash that would eventually come into my life, but I cannot blame my friends and relationships for where I ended up. I only have myself to blame because I chose them. In many cases, we blame our friends and relationships when bad things happen to us, but ultimately we chose to embrace those friends and it was us who gave them the power they had over our lives. It is important to understand that people choose who they believe and trust just like when a young person starts hanging out with the wrong crowd, they did it by choice, no one makes them choose those relationships. The fact that we are choosing the wrong relationships needs to serve as a sign that there is something wrong in our lives.

I was setting in a restaurant a few years ago and my waitress recognized me from my television ministry and asked, "Are you Pastor Lance

Johnson?" I shared with her that I was. She seemed to be in some sort of inner struggle as she proceeded to take my order. After taking my order she came back to my table and asked if I thought a homosexual could be a Christian? I responded by asking her if a person who was a Christian could be involved in an adulterous affair? Her reply was yes I guess so and with a puzzled look she walked away. Shortly after she brought my food and set down at my table and proceeded to tell me about her friend who was a homosexual. She said she was born that way but still felt guilty about the fact she was involved in a same sex relationship. I began by telling her that we are all born with a sinful nature according to Romans 5 and that all people sin in some way, and most have a sin of choice. The sin of that person's choice was homosexuality just like the sin of my choice, while in the world, was drugs. I explained that everyone sins, but different people choose to commit different sins. Also that it was in every person's nature to sin because of the fall of man. I went on to explain to her that Jesus died so we could be forgiven of sin, but that He also through the power of the Holy Spirit gave us the power to be changed so that we could be delivered from the power sin has over our lives.

*2 Corinthians 5:17 (KJV) Therefore if any man be in Christ, he is a new creature: old things are passed away; behold, all things are become new.*

I went on to share with her that many times the church judges sin as if it has degrees, but that sin is sin no matter what kind it is and God would forgive this person and deliver them if they would allow Him to. At that moment, the girl began to weep and confessed she was the person in question and it was her who was involved in homosexuality. She then repented and asked God to forgive her and deliver her from her sin. That same day she came to our Wednesday evening service and sat on the front row a changed person.

For too long the church has judged people because of the type of sin a person has been involved with, as if some sin was so bad that God could not forgive, change, and heal them. Jesus himself ministered to those people that were so vile they did not deserve forgiveness or the opportunity to be changed. He ministered to those caught in the act of adultery, a woman who was a notorious sinner with a reputation to back it up and a woman who had been divorced and remarried five times and shacking up with a man, at the time he ministered to her. Sin is sin and it all has consequences in this life and in eternity. This is the reason we need a savior. The guilt that the prodigal son felt made him ashamed and fearful of returning to his father, but he knew he could not stay in the pig pen any longer. I lived under the assumption that my sin and lifestyle was so bad I could not turn to God because of all I had done. I had heard preachers say that God's Spirit would not always tarry with a man and if a person went to long he or she could not be forgiven. The very shame of who I was and what I had done, along with the fear of what people would think, and the fear of being rejected by God kept me from turning to God. Even though I knew I needed His help. One of the greatest deceptions the enemy uses to keep us in our sin is his ability to stand as our accuser (Revelations 12:10). Well meaning people can become the devil's advocate by standing in judgment of people because of what they have done. The prodigal son's older brother is a great example of the attitude a person can have toward someone who has been involved in a vile sinful lifestyle. He did not think it was right for his father to forgive and restore his brother because of his rebellious lifestyle. Another example, Simon the Pharisee when he judged the woman who came into his house and fell at the feet of Jesus, washing his feet with her hair and anointing Him with oil. He stated that if Jesus would have known what kind of woman she was he would not be allowing her to do so, but He knew exactly what kind of woman she was and he declared this when he told her that her sins, which were MANY, were forgiven. My perception of how God would receive me was based upon how I had seen people treat those with a background similar to mine, and because of that, I continued to remain in the bondage of sin.

Today people are raised very differently with a diversity of moral standards. For instance, one person could be taught moral standards as relates to the bible. Where another person may be raised where there is no understanding of the bible and the only moral standard is the one given by several generations of family members. Who for example, may have been alcoholics, drug users, prostitutes and thieves. Regardless of how they were raised and taught they are still born with a sinful nature and are in need of being born again. The Pharisees of Jesus day were moral but they were not born again; their nature had not changed. My greatest battle with sin was the fact that I enjoyed it and because of that I did not think I could come to God. When our nature is sinful, sin is what we desire and for a season it feels so good. For some drugs are not desirable but for others it is, for some stealing is not a desire but for others it is. For others it may be strife, envy or jealousy but for others it is not. I have met good moral people who would never drink, partake of drugs, cheat on their spouse or even curse but they live to gossip. My point is, that every person is born with that sinful nature and sin is what a person will desire even though the types of sin people commit are as different as the hairstyles they choose. The scriptures teach us in Romans 3:23 that all have sinned and come short of the Glory of God and that we are all in need of a savior regardless of what sins we have chosen to partake of. Since we all need a savior, never let what people say or think about you be a reason not to come to Jesus. It is important for you to know that Jesus said He did not come into the world for those that are well but those that are sick in their sins.

It appeared to me that I was living the ultimate life, partying, having fun, and doing things my way. I was surrounded with pleasure on every side until one day it all began to change. A series of events would begin to transpire in my life that would take me where I never thought I would go. Those events are like a blur to me and the order in which they occurred seem to run together, but I will do my best to give you a glimpse into what happened. It started with being pulled over by the police one Sunday afternoon after spending the whole day partying on the lake. I was arrested with multiple charges, amongst them were a DUI and possession of controlled substances. I some how escaped felony charges but paid out a whole lot of money in fines and attorney fees. Later I would end up in bankruptcy and losing all my material possessions, all due to my addiction to alcohol, cocaine and the lifestyle that accompanied it. I lost my business, my cars, and my high rolling life was gone. I will never forget the feeling I felt when my pride was deflated. The day the bank repossessed my cars I went from having everything to having nothing in what seemed to me, a matter of moments. When you go from having everything you want, to not being able to buy diapers for your child, it becomes a wake up call. My world was crashing down around me and to make things worse I resorted to getting high to help me deal with the loss and feelings of failure. Not long after, my wife came to a place she could not take any more and left with our daughter. Even though we had separated many times, I knew this time was for good. I became very suicidal and depressed. To feel comforted my dependency on drugs and alcohol intensified. My desire to live was gone. I fell into such a state of hopelessness that it is impossible for me to describe. I was faced with the reality that I had destroyed my family, lost everything, burned all my relationships, and all I had to show for it was a two hundred and fifty dollar per day cocaine habit. I was faced with the fact that I was an alcoholic and had no job or family to turn to. All of this should have been my pig pen experience where I woke up, but instead I got worse and so did everything around me. I went what seemed like an eternity without a moment of being sober. Looking back, I believe I was trying to kill myself with a drug and alcohol over dose. During this delirious time, I spent every moment with my best friend. We were both going through some of the same problems, so we just thought we could deal with them by partying. He was the only person who knew about my inner turmoil because I had shared with him openly about my feelings of despair. I had even talked with him about my experiences with God as a child. I realize now that God was trying with all His power to reach me at the most difficult time in my life, but I refused to say yes to His plan. Then the most tragic thing that could have happened, did. My best friend committed suicide, the one person I had left in my life was gone. I cannot remember the days following his death. I was totally numb and in a state of incoherency. For those reading this book I must warn you, sin has a pay check and its agenda will be revealed in the end. The wages of sin are death and death is where I was. I was a walking dead man because everything that represented life to me at that time was now dead. My home, business, marriage, family, finances, future, and my best friend were all gone. The prodigal son did not come to himself until he ended up in the pig pen. The pig pen is the point a person reaches where they are as low as they can possibly go without being physically dead. It is the place that becomes a turning point or a wakeup call for someone. I wish to this day I would have come to my pig pen much earlier in my journey but unfortunately for me, I had to go even deeper into the mud. In the midst of all this despair and confusion I felt God calling me. I even felt Him drawing me and warning me through secular songs. I was being pursued and there was no place to run or hide. I could not get high enough on drugs or alcohol to escape God. I could not escape the memories of all the times my brother Mark had tried to tell me about Jesus and being born again. His words would echo over and over in my mind. The one thing that caused me to deny the words my brother had spoken and the feelings I was experiencing, was the fact that I believed in Jesus and had actually prayed the sinner's prayer and was baptized as a teenager. I thought I was saved because of what I was told. The fact is, I did believe in Jesus but I had never actually repented of my sins and given my life to God. Religion became a stumbling block for me because I was told I was saved. When in actuality I had never been truly born-again. Despite the fact that I thought I was saved did not silence God from calling me to Himself. The pain and the calling of God were all colliding in my head and things finally came to boiling point September 2, 1990, in the living room of my home in Lake Arrowhead. In a terrible state of mind, I felt the only way out was to kill myself and that's what I would attempt to do. I grabbed my Smith & Wesson 357 magnum and placed it to my temple while shaking profusely. All I could think of was the tragedy I spoke of in an earlier chapter that I blamed God for. That tragedy was the suicide of my Grandfather and that event had affected my life beyond my ability to put in words. I was there as a young boy of 10 years old and witnessed this tragic event. I saw first-hand the pain that it caused all of my family for so many years. One other thing that kept going through my mind, that was ultimately the determining factor for the following events, was the fear that I would go to hell if I pulled the trigger. Before I tell you the events that followed I want to tell you why I feared hell. Religious people can sometimes be very cruel and insensitive. While at the funeral home during viewing hours I overheard people saying that a person who commits suicide goes to hell. Those words devastated me as a young boy and the thought of my Grandfather in hell never left my mind. Although now as a student of the word of God I found out those people were very much wrong in their statement but nevertheless it became the reason I did not pull the trigger of that 357 magnum that was pointed at my head. At that very moment with gun in hand the greatest battle of my life began. I begin to cry out to God and in that one-sided conversation I began to go through every emotion that could be experienced with an intensity like never before. I screamed at God with anger and rage, I cried with humility and brokenness. I cried and spoke with great pain and confusion, but what stands out so clear in my memory was the honesty I spoke to God with. I held nothing back that night in that great battle I was having with God. I told Him how I like the things I was doing that were so sinful and how they felt good and how I enjoyed them. I also told Him how they were destroying my life and taking everything I loved and cared for away from me. I also told God I did not have the power to quit those things or change, but that I truly did want to, because that lifestyle of sin was costing more than I ever wanted to pay. I remember feeling completely numb after what seemed like hours of wrestling with God. I went and found my bible that my Pastor had given me after my Grandfathers death. I knew very little about the bible but I knew the words in red were the words of Jesus. As I searched through the bible for some red letters, the first scriptures I found were *Matthew 16:24-25 (NLT) Then Jesus said to his disciples, "If any of you wants to be my follower, you must turn from your selfish ways, take up your cross, and follow me. If you try to hang on to your life, you will lose it. But if you give up your life for my sake, you will save it.* When I read that scripture I knew exactly what it meant and it was as if God Himself spoke to me and said, son I want your whole life and nothing less. At that very moment I told God that He could have my whole life and I would do anything He wanted me to do. All I asked was for Him to change my life and take away the desire for all those sins I had clung to for so long, that had destroyed my life. One of the things I haven't shared with you yet is the fact that during my Grandfather's funeral I felt God calling me to preach. That calling never left my mind from that day. As a young boy I spoke with my Pastor about it but later tried to dismiss and abandon the very thought of it although, nothing I did would allow me to escape that feeling. Even though, in my journey of sin, I doubted the very existence of God that called and pulled at me everyday of my life. That night in my living room I became willing to give God my entire life and that meant I would preach if that was what God wanted for my life. That night I asked God to forgive me and pleaded with him to have mercy on me through Jesus Christ and I at that moment died to my own will and to myself.

I believe that there are people who are reading this book that may be where I once was and you too would like to be changed. I am here as a witness and to provide proof that God can truly change your life if you are willing to surrender your life to Him and accept Jesus Christ as your savior and Lord. There is no sin you have committed that the blood Jesus shed for you cannot forgive. There is no bondage or sin in your life that God cannot deliver you from. You may ask, what must I do to experience this kind of change in my life?

The answer is simple, you must truly repent of your sins and this means more than just feeling sorry for your sins. You must understand what sin is doing to you and truly desire to rid it from your life. This is called repentance and the scriptures teach us that if we will repent of our sins God will forgive us and change us.

*Acts 3:19 (KJV) Repent ye therefore, and be converted, that your sins may be blotted out, when the times of refreshing shall come from the presence of the Lord;*

You must believe with all your heart that Jesus Christ died and shed His blood for your sins and you must also believe that God raised Him from the grave on the third day.

*Romans 10:9-11 (NLT) If you confess with your mouth that Jesus is Lord and believe in your heart that God raised him from the dead, you will be saved. For it is by believing in your heart that you are made right with God, and it is by confessing with your mouth that you are saved. As the Scriptures tell us, "Anyone who trusts in him will never be disgraced."*

You must also surrender your will and life to Jesus as Lord of your life. This means you must be willing to live for Him and follow Him as Lord of your life. It means His will for your life is more important to you than anything or anyone including yourself.

*Luke 9:23-26 (NLT) Then he said to the crowd, "If any of you wants to be my follower, you must turn from your selfish ways, take up your cross daily, and follow me. If you try to hang on to your life, you will lose it. But if you give up your life for my sake, you will save it. And what do you benefit if you gain the whole world but are yourself lost or destroyed? If anyone is ashamed of me and my message, the Son of Man will be ashamed of that person when he returns in his glory and in the glory of the Father and the holy angels.*

The night of the great battle with God when I finally surrendered all and declared to God you win, was the beginning of the greatest miracle I have ever experienced which was the change that would take place in my life in the days to come. That night I did not feel changed, I did not experience a feeling that I had changed, I was simply numb and just wanted to go to bed. So that night I put my pistol on the shelf and my bible back on the bookcase and went to bed not realizing what had taken place in my life. The next day I got up and went to work as I always did. My morning routine consisted of me going by the convenient store and picking up a case of beer. On this day however, something profound happened. I walked into the store and went straight to the beer cooler like I always did, but when I went to open the door I couldn't. I stood at the cooler door and had an argument with myself. I walked out of the store that day empty handed. Later that day I went to smoke a cigarette and could not strike the lighter to light the cigarette. After lunch my buddies called to see if we were going out to the club that night and to my surprise I immediately said no. Something was happening to me, I was experiencing for the first time real conviction and power to do what was right and resist the wrong that I had done for so long. I continued that day to say no to all the sins that I was once so addicted to, and had indulged in for so much of my life. My language changed and my attitude changed to the point that people wanted to know what was wrong with me. I eventually told everyone that God had done something in my life and I was no longer interested in my old lifestyle. That stand in particular removed most of my friends. The truth is, none of my old friends wanted anything to do with me and they avoided me at all cost. My wife returned home and we began the process of healing. She had to learn how to live with a man she had never known before because I was certainly very different than the person she married. We immediately started going to church and the pastor quickly became my closest friend and he began disciplining me on a personal level. I had a new passion for God that could not be quenched, and it was growing more and more powerful by the day. Although I was growing and changing daily, people were very skeptical of me and really doubted the change that had taken place in my life. Many criticized me and talked behind my back. My own family did not understand this change and feared it would be short lived. I was extremely controversial in the church I attended because I had publicly confessed my call to the ministry and many of the leaders of that church did not think I was or could ever be qualified to preach the gospel. As I write this book, I have been saved and have been serving the Lord for twenty-five years and people still do not believe I have changed. They are still skeptical and spread false rumors about me. I must admit, I was hurt by all the things people said about me and did to me. I was so passionate for God, I found the grace and strength from God to forgive them and continue my pursuit of God and His will for my life, even to this day. I became a devout student of the word and I eventually began taking correspondent courses from Liberty University. When a person gives their life to serve God they become a threat to the devil, and he certainly will do all that he can to discourage you and cause you to quit. If you look for a reason to quit and go back, you can find one. Some of the meanest people I have ever encountered are in the church, but the fact is I wake up everyday and look for a reason to continue on in the will of God. I will not allow the devil to discourage me from the things of God such as; the church, godly fellowship, praise, and the Word of God because all of these are tools God uses to edify us everyday and help us grow spiritually. Remember, we are to die to our self-daily and continue to follow God. We cannot use the old excuses we used when were lost, as to why we don't serve God, because now as a true follower of Christ that has been born-again we know better. I encourage you today to make up your mind that you will not let anything that the devil does or people do discourage you from doing God's will. If I had quit I would have never had the joy of seeing all the wonderful things that God has done through my life. The truth is, I was never qualified for the ministry but the blood of Jesus qualified me. I was never capable of doing what the Lord called me to do but the power of the Holy Spirit made me capable. I have had the privilege of leading thousands to Jesus over the years. I have built churches all over the world, established bible colleges in many countries, built Christian rehabs, written books and preached all over the world. Not one of these things would have happened if I would have found a reason to quit. You cannot look back but you must look forward to the plan and purpose God has for your life.

# ABOUT THE AUTHOR

Lance Johnson comes by way of a life of struggles, having been trapped by the unrelenting grip of alcohol and drug addiction and the desperate lifestyle that comes with it. He brings a fresh word that is woven into the fabric of a life that has known the agony of an empty soul.

One early fall day in September of 1990 he had an encounter with the King of Kings that not only changed him but has eternally altered the lives of thousands who now proclaim along with him that "When Jesus sets you free you are completely free." Lance now reaches into the depths of his experience to deliver a starkly real story of freedom by the power of God. Now he only looks back to encourage those who are lagging behind. He has spent almost a quarter of a century rescuing people from death and ruin by introducing them to a life of prosperity and liberty.

Lance has pioneered addiction recovery ministries as well as numerous churches. He has planted Bible colleges and overseas mission works, thereby reaching people from every walk of life and social background. He has introduced vast numbers of people to a victorious, overcoming lifestyle. After twenty-four years of ministering to people struggling with addiction, he has reduced his experience and knowledge to the pages of this book. This work is not a twelve-step recovery program. In fact, this book is not about recovery at all; it is about something far greater than recovery—it is about complete liberty. Freedom not only from addiction, but freedom from the inward condition that caused it. The best that man can offer in addiction recovery is a 10 percent success rate. As this book didn't come from man, it promises a miraculous 100 percent success rate. If you follow its teachings, success will happen.

Lance Johnson is the Founder and Overseer of the Relevate Family of Churches, with various locations in North Georgia and Ghana, West Africa. He is also the founder and overseer of Lions Gate Ministry Training Academy and REVAMP School of Transformation. He resides in Woodstock, Georgia, with his wife, Lisa. They have two adult children, Brittany and Marcus, and one granddaughter, Makenlee.

# CHAPTER 1

## Repentance

The Greek word metanoeō translates as "repent," and means to think differently or afterward, for instance, to reconsider.

To REPENT means you must begin to think differently. It means that you must make up your mind that you are going to change and do differently.

The Scripture states in Acts 3:19 (KJV), "Repent ye therefore, and be converted, that your sins may be blotted out, when the times of refreshing shall come from the presence of the Lord." Repentance brings conversion. The word CONVERTED in Acts 3:19 in the Greek is epistrephō, meaning to turn around and do differently, and can be translated to "changed."

To sum up, repentance is to say that you make up your mind that you are going to change and do differently.

Repentance is not just feeling sorry for what you have done; it is an action of changing your mind and actually changing your behavior. It means that you are going to do an about-face and go in the other direction. If you are unwilling to allow your life to go in a new direction, then you have not repented.

Repentance in and of itself can do nothing. The key to repenting from your old life is turning to Jesus Christ and the life He alone can provide and has chosen for you. In John 12:23-26 (NLT), "Jesus replied, 'Now the time has come for the Son of Man to enter into His glory. I tell you the truth, unless a kernel of wheat is planted in the soil and dies, it remains alone. But its death will produce many new kernels—a plentiful harvest of new lives. Those who love their life in this world will lose it. Those who care nothing for their life in this world will keep it for eternity. Anyone who wants to be my disciple must follow me, because my servants must be where I am. And the Father will honor anyone who serves me.'"

Jesus has given us His life, but to accept it we must be spiritually born-again. John 3:3 tells us about this miraculous conversion in which our lives are forever changed. Our spirit becomes changed into the Spirit

1

that is like His. In John 3:3-7 (NLT), "Jesus replied, 'I tell you the truth, unless you are born again, you cannot see the Kingdom of God.' 'What do You mean?' exclaimed Nicodemus. 'How can an old man go back into his mother's womb and be born again?' Jesus replied, 'I assure you, no one can enter the Kingdom of God without being born of water and the Spirit. Humans can reproduce only human life, but the Holy Spirit gives birth to spiritual life. So don't be surprised when I say, 'You must be born again.'"

Romans 8:9 (NLT) tells us that we are not controlled by our sinful nature. We are controlled by the Spirit if we have the Spirit of God living in us. (And remember that those who do not have the Spirit of Christ living in them do not belong to Him at all.)

According to 2 Corinthians 5:17 (NLT), "This means that anyone who belongs to Christ has become a new person. The old life is gone; a new life has begun!"

"Don't copy the behavior and customs of this world, but let God transform you into a new person by changing the way you think. Then you will learn to know God's will for you, which is good and pleasing and perfect" (Rom 12:2 NLT).

Transformation is an event, but it is also a continual change that takes place as we follow Jesus.

Following Jesus is not an option but an absolute must if you expect to become free from addiction and remain free.

Because our new life (behavior, understanding, perspectives, lifestyle) is in Christ, we must walk in Him.

> And now, just as you accepted Christ Jesus as your Lord, you must continue to follow Him. Let your roots grow down into Him, and let your lives be built on Him. Then your faith will grow strong in the truth you were taught, and you will overflow with thankfulness.
>
> Don't let anyone capture you with empty philosophies and high-sounding nonsense that come from human thinking and from the spiritual powers of this world, rather than from Christ. For in Christ lives all the fullness of God in a human body. So you also are complete through your union with Christ, who is the head over every ruler and authority.

2

When you came to Christ, you were "circumcised," but not by a physical procedure. Christ performed a spiritual circumcision—the cutting away of your sinful nature. For you were buried with Christ when you were baptized. And with Him you were raised to new life because you trusted the mighty power of God, who raised Christ from the dead. (Col 2:6-12 NLT)

"This is the message we have heard from Him and declare to you: God is light; in Him there is no darkness at all. If we claim to have fellowship with Him yet walk in the darkness, we lie and do not live by the truth. But if we walk in the light, as He is in the light, we have fellowship with one another, and the blood of Jesus, His Son, purifies us from all sin" (1 Jn 1:5-7 NIV).

Although many have said addiction is a disease, it is more! Addiction is a sin. According to Scripture, sin kills and that is what addiction has been doing to those who fall victim to it. It kills your dreams, your hopes, your relationships, and everything that is valuable. The most significant thing is that it kills you spiritually. It kills the life and purpose God created you for. We will study this in much greater detail in later chapters.

The only cure for sin is Jesus Christ and what He accomplished for us through His death and Resurrection. Jesus through regeneration (Being Born-Again) broke the power of sin over our life.

"When you were slaves to sin, you were free from the obligation to do right. And what was the result? You are now ashamed of the things you used to do, things that end in eternal doom. But now you are free from the power of sin and have become slaves of God. Now you do those things that lead to holiness and result in eternal life. For the wages of sin is death, but the free gift of God is eternal life through Christ Jesus our Lord" (Rom 6:20-23 NLT).

Jesus's death on the cross provided atonement and forgiveness for the sins we have committed and the sins we will commit. This forgiveness is so we no longer have to live in the guilt and shame of what we have done, but it has a much greater purpose. It provided forgiveness so we could have access to God and constant fellowship with Him. The blood Jesus shed for us has provided the cleansing of our lives so that God through the Holy Spirit could come and dwell in you and me. God now becomes more than just the creator of heaven and earth; He now becomes our God and we become His children. The blood provided the forgiveness so that He can now indwell our once-unclean lives and bring to us the strength and ability to overcome the power of sin that held us bound. Below are some Scripture references showing the results of what Jesus did for us through His death and resurrection.

"If you love me, obey my commandments. And I will ask the Father, and He will give you another Advocate, who will never leave you. He is the Holy Spirit, who leads into all truth. The world cannot receive Him because it isn't looking for Him and doesn't recognize him. But you know Him because He lives with you now and later will be in you. No, I will not abandon you as orphans—I will come to you. Soon the world will no longer see me, but you will see me. Since I live, you also will live. When I am raised to life again, you will know that I am in my Father, and you are in Me, and I am in you. Those who accept my commandments and obey them are the ones who love Me. And because they love Me, My Father will love them. And I will love them and reveal Myself to each of them."

Judas (not Judas Iscariot, but the other disciple with that name) said to Him, "Lord, why are You going to reveal Yourself only to us and not to the world at large?"

Jesus replied, "All who love Me will do what I say. My Father will love them, and We will come and make Our home with each of them" (Jn 14:15-23 NLT).

But now God has shown us a way to be made right with Him without keeping the requirements of the law, as was promised in the writings of Moses and the prophets long ago. We are made right with God by placing our faith in Jesus Christ. And this is true for everyone who believes, no matter who we are.

For everyone has sinned; we all fall short of God's glorious standard. Yet God, with undeserved kindness, declares that we are righteous. He did this through Christ Jesus when He freed us from the penalty for our sins. For God presented Jesus as the sacrifice for sin. People are made right with God when they believe that Jesus sacrificed His life, shedding His blood. This sacrifice shows that God was being fair when He held back and did not punish those who sinned in times past, for He was looking ahead and including them in what He would do in this present time. God did this to demonstrate His righteousness, for He Himself is fair and just, and He declares sinners to be right in His sight when they believe in Jesus. (Rom 3:21-26 NLT)

From 1 Corinthians 6:19-20 (NLT): "Don't you realize that your body is the temple of the Holy Spirit, who lives in you and was given to you by God? You do not belong to yourself, for God bought you with a high price. So you must honor God with your body."

# CHAPTER 2

## The Cost of Following Jesus

Most people say salvation is free; that is not necessarily true. Although Jesus dying for us is free, to follow Him is not. That is one of the key elements to being free from addiction—to follow Him is very expensive and comes with the ultimate price. The cost of following Jesus is you giving up your life. Your life consists of more than the air you breathe and your existence in this world. Your life is yourself as you know it. This includes things like your old habits and mannerisms, social life, hobbies, reputation, dreams, and aspirations. It can even include relationships and financial status. Your life consists of everything that makes up who you are. God wants you to lose your life so that He can give you His life. Matthew 16:25 (KJV): "For whosoever will save his life shall lose it: and whosoever will lose his life for My sake shall find it."

Jesus taught us to count the cost before we decide to follow Him. When people don't count the cost, it results in their failure and is exactly why so many people relapse and stumble in their efforts to be free from addiction.

Luke 14:25-35 (NLT) tells us:

A large crowd was following Jesus. He turned around and said to them, "If you want to be My disciple, you must, by comparison, hate everyone else—your father and mother, wife and children, brothers and sisters—yes, even your own life. Otherwise, you cannot be My disciple. And if you do not carry your own cross and follow Me, you cannot be My disciple.

But don't begin until you count the cost. For who would begin construction of a building without first calculating the cost to see if there is enough money to finish it? Otherwise, you might complete only the foundation before running out of money, and then everyone would laugh at you. They would say, 'There's the person who started that building and couldn't afford to finish it!'

Or what king would go to war against another king without first sitting down with his counselors to discuss whether

7

his army of 10,000 could defeat the 20,000 soldiers marching against him? And if he can't, he will send a delegation to discuss terms of peace while the enemy is still far away. So you cannot become my disciple without giving up everything you own.

Salt is good for seasoning. But if it loses its flavor, how do you make it salty again? Flavorless salt is good neither for the soil nor for the manure pile. It is thrown away. Anyone with ears to hear should listen and understand!"

Jesus is very clear when He explained the price of following Him, and He never made an-exception for anyone as it relates to that cost. If we are unwilling to pay that cost, then we cannot be His disciple. Let's take a look at the cost. According to Matthew 16:24-27 (KJV), "Then said Jesus unto His disciples, 'If any man will come after Me, let him deny himself, and take up his cross, and follow Me. For whosoever will save his life shall lose it: and whosoever will lose his life for My sake shall find it. For what is a man profited, if he shall gain the whole world, and lose his own soul? or what shall a man give in exchange for his soul? For the Son of man shall come in the glory of his Father with his angels; and then He shall reward every man according to his works.'"

In Luke, "As they were walking along, someone said to Jesus, 'I will follow You wherever You go.' But Jesus replied, 'Foxes have dens to live in, and birds have nests, but the Son of Man has no place even to lay his head.' He said to another person, 'Come, follow Me.' The man agreed, but he said, 'Lord, first let me return home and bury my father.' But Jesus told him, 'Let the spiritually dead bury their own dead! Your duty is to go and preach about the Kingdom of God.' Another said, 'Yes, Lord, I will follow You, but first let me say good-bye to my family.' But Jesus told him, 'Anyone who puts a hand to the plow and then looks back is not fit for the Kingdom of God.'" (9:57-62 NLT).

The Scriptures provide us with examples of people who sought Jesus but refused to pay the price of following Him and left disappointed. One of the greatest examples is the Rich Young Ruler.

Someone came to Jesus with this question: "Teacher, what good deed must I do to have eternal life?"

"Why ask Me about what is good?" Jesus replied. "There is only One who is good. But to answer your question—if you want to receive eternal life, keep the commandments."

"Which ones?" the man asked.

And Jesus replied: "You must not murder. You must not commit adultery. You must not steal. You must not testify falsely. Honor your father and mother. Love your neighbor as yourself."

"I've obeyed all these commandments," the young man replied. "What else must I do?"

Jesus told him, "If you want to be perfect, go and sell all your possessions and give the money to the poor, and you will have treasure in heaven. Then come, follow Me."

But when the young man heard this, he went away very sad, for he had many possessions. (Mt 19:16-22 NLT)

It was not the wealth of this man that prevented Him from following God, but it was his love for his wealth. He loved his wealth more than he loved God.

If his wealth had not been what controlled his life and his decision, then he would have been able to receive the life he was looking for. Instead of obeying what Jesus told him, he allowed his wealth to dictate his obedience and decision because it was more important to him than Jesus. In a nutshell, his wealth was Lord of his life and not Jesus.

"Not everyone who calls out to Me, 'Lord! Lord!' will enter the Kingdom of Heaven. Only those who actually do the will of My Father in heaven will enter" (Mt 7:21 NLT).

Jesus will only ask you to give Him what you love more than Him.

# CHAPTER 3

## You Cannot Love This World

The word of God is very clear about forbidding us to love this world and the things that are of this world. The reason for this is they become idols in our lives that can easily become more valued than the will of God being done in our lives. When we begin to develop a love for this world and the things in this world, we will then begin to regress in the change God is working in our lives.

"Do not love this world nor the things it offers you, for when you love the world, you do not have the love of the Father in you. For the world offers only a craving for physical pleasure, a craving for everything we see, and pride in our achievements and possessions. These are not from the Father, but are from this world. And this world is fading away, along with everything that people crave. But anyone who does what pleases God will live forever" (1 Jn 2:15-17 NLT).

Because Satan is the god of this world (the worldly system), it is his great tool to allure you away from God and His will being done in your life, which ultimately robs you of the new life Jesus Christ has provided for you.

"Satan, who is the god of this world, has blinded the minds of those who don't believe. They are unable to see the glorious light of the Good News. They don't understand this message about the glory of Christ, who is the exact likeness of God" (2 Cor 4:4 NLT).

Once you were dead because of your disobedience and your many sins. You used to live in sin, just like the rest of the world, obeying the devil—the commander of the powers in the unseen world. He is the spirit at work in the hearts of those who refuse to obey God. All of us used to live that way, following the passionate desires and inclinations of our sinful nature. By our very nature we were subject to God's anger, just like everyone else.

But God is so rich in mercy, and He loved us so much, that even though we were dead because of our sins, He gave us life when He raised Christ from the dead. (It is only by God's grace that you have been saved!) For He raised us from the dead along with Christ and seated us with Him in the heavenly realms because we are united with Christ Jesus. So God can point to us in all future ages as examples of the incredible wealth of His grace and kindness toward us, as shown in all He has done for us who are united with Christ Jesus. (Eph 2:1-7 NLT)

The Scriptures show us how Satan tempts us with the things of this world, attempting to cause us to walk away from the will of God for our lives. It demonstrates this in the temptation of Jesus in the wilderness.

Then Jesus was led by the Spirit into the wilderness to be tempted there by the devil. For forty days and forty nights He fasted and became very hungry.

During that time the devil came and said to Him, "If You are the Son of God, tell these stones to become loaves of bread."

But Jesus told him, "No! The Scriptures say,

'People do not live by bread alone,

but by every word that comes from the mouth of God.'

Then the devil took Him to the holy city, Jerusalem, to the highest point of the Temple, and said, "If You are the Son of God, jump off! For the Scriptures say,

'He will order His angels to protect You.

And they will hold You up with their hands

so You won't even hurt Your foot on a stone.'

Jesus responded, "The Scriptures also say, 'You must not test the LORD your God.'"

Next the devil took Him to the peak of a very high mountain and showed Him all the kingdoms of the world and their glory. "I will give it all to You," he said, "if You will kneel down and worship me."

"Get out of here, Satan," Jesus told him. "For the Scriptures say,

'You must worship the LORD your God

and serve only Him.'"

Then the devil went away, and angels came and took care of Jesus. (Mt 4:1-11 NLT)

Satan tempted Jesus in three different ways with the things of this world.

1.  Jesus was hungry, and Satan tempted Him with bread. He tried to get Him to use His power to turn stones into bread when He should be fasting. Jesus had the power to do this, but it wasn't the will of God. Just because we have the power and ability to meet a need in our life doesn't mean it is the will of God. An example of this in our life would be putting a job in front of church, ministry, and moral decisions.

2.  He tempted Jesus to prove His Sonship through a miracle. Satan uses our pride to cause us to do things that are not the will of God. You have nothing to prove to anyone as it relates to who you are in Christ or especially trying to live up to someone's expectations as it relates to the old person you used to be.

3.  The third temptation was one that we all face—when Satan tried to get Jesus to bow down to his will instead of God's will. He offered Him wealth, power, and popularity if He would only bow down and worship him. Worship is yielding one's self and allegiance to another. Satan is always telling us what we could have or what we could be if we would just yield ourselves to him instead of God.

# CHAPTER 4

## Sin and Its Agenda

As mentioned in an earlier chapter, addiction is not a sickness but a sin. To understand addiction, you must understand sin and what it intends to do to you. Once you understand sin and its agenda, you will actually hate it and want nothing to do with it.

Sin is more than a list of dos and don'ts. It is not doing the will of God in your life, and that is what Satan uses to tempt us and allure us out of the will of God. "Look here, you who say, 'Today or tomorrow we are going to a certain town and will stay there a year. We will do business there and make a profit.' How do you know what your life will be like tomorrow? Your life is like the morning fog—it's here a little while, then it's gone. What you ought to say is, 'If the Lord wants us to, we will live and do this or that.' Otherwise you are boasting about your own plans, and all such boasting is evil. Remember, it is sin to know what you ought to do and then not do it" (Jas 4:13-17 NLT).

Satan is the author of sin, and it is his greatest weapon against you to pull you away from your devotion and obedience to God. "For I am jealous for you with the jealousy of God himself. I promised you as a pure bride to one husband—Christ. But I fear that somehow your pure and undivided devotion to Christ will be corrupted, just as Eve was deceived by the cunning ways of the serpent" (2 Cor 11:2-3 NLT).

Sin's agenda is to enslave you and control you so that you will not obey God and experience the abundant life He has provided for you.

According to Romans 6:5-19 (NLT):

Since we have been united with Him in His death, we will also be raised to life as He was. We know that our old sinful selves were crucified with Christ so that sin might lose its power in our lives. We are no longer slaves to sin. For when we died with Christ we were set free from the power of sin. And since we died with Christ, we know we will also live with Him. We are sure of this because Christ was raised from the dead, and He will never die again. Death no longer has any power over Him. When He died, He died once to break the power of sin. But now that He lives, He lives for the glory of God. So you also should consider

15

yourselves to be dead to the power of sin and alive to God through Christ Jesus.

Do not let sin control the way you live; do not give in to sinful desires. Do not let any part of your body become an instrument of evil to serve sin. Instead, give yourselves completely to God, for you were dead, but now you have new life. So use your whole body as an instrument to do what is right for the glory of God. Sin is no longer your master, for you no longer live under the requirements of the law. Instead, you live under the freedom of God's grace.

Well then, since God's grace has set us free from the law, does that mean we can go on sinning? Of course not! Don't you realize that you become the slave of whatever you choose to obey? You can be a slave to sin, which leads to death, or you can choose to obey God, which leads to righteous living. Thank God! Once you were slaves of sin, but now you wholeheartedly obey this teaching we have given you. Now you are free from your slavery to sin, and you have become slaves to righteous living.

Because of the weakness of your human nature, I am using the illustration of slavery to help you understand all this. Previously, you let yourselves be slaves to impurity and lawlessness, which led ever deeper into sin. Now you must give yourselves to be slaves to righteous living so that you will become holy.

2 Peter 2:19-22 (NLT) tells us: "They promise freedom, but they themselves are slaves of sin and corruption. For you are a slave to whatever controls you. And when people escape from the wickedness of the world by knowing our Lord and Savior Jesus Christ and then get tangled up and enslaved by sin again, they are worse off than before. It would be better if they had never known the way to righteousness than to know it and then reject the command they were given to live a holy life. They prove the truth of this proverb: 'A dog returns to its vomit.' And another says, 'A washed pig returns to the mud.'"

The good news is that Jesus Christ destroyed the works of sin that the devil uses against us! It is simply up to us to choose by the grace and strength of God to do the will of God.

And you know that Jesus came to take away our sins, and there is no sin in Him. Anyone who continues to live in Him will not sin. But anyone who keeps on sinning does not know Him or understand who He is.

Dear children, don't let anyone deceive you about this: When people do what is right, it shows that they are righteous, even as Christ is righteous. But when people keep on sinning, it shows that they belong to the devil, who has been sinning since the beginning. But the Son of God came to destroy the works of the devil. Those who have been born into God's family do not make a practice of sinning because God's life is in them. So they can't keep on sinning because they are children of God. So now we can tell who are children of God and who are children of the devil. Anyone who does not live righteously and does not love other believers does not belong to God. (1 Jn 3:5-10 NLT)

# CHAPTER 5

Spiritual Maturity (Growing Up)

Spiritual maturity does not happen by itself like physical maturity; it takes an effort on our part, or it will never happen. Spiritual maturity is the key to a life free of addictions. It is costly but worth every sacrifice made to obtain it.

Spiritual maturity is accomplished by faithfully following Christ as we have already studied in an earlier chapter; without following Him daily it can never be achieved. As we follow Christ, spiritual maturity takes place and change is the result. We change from the old person we once were to the image and reflection of Christ Jesus, which is what the Bible describes as the new man.

According to Ephesians 4:17-24 (NLT), "With the Lord's authority I say this: Live no longer as the Gentiles do, for they are hopelessly confused. Their minds are full of darkness; they wander far from the life God gives because they have closed their minds and hardened their hearts against him. They have no sense of shame. They live for lustful pleasure and eagerly practice every kind of impurity. But that isn't what you learned about Christ. Since you have heard about Jesus and have learned the truth that comes from Him, throw off your old sinful nature and your former way of life, which is corrupted by lust and deception. Instead, let the Spirit renew your thoughts and attitudes. Put on your new nature, created to be like God—truly righteous and holy."

In Colossians 3:5-10 (NLT), we are told, "So put to death the sinful, earthly things lurking within you. Have nothing to do with sexual immorality, impurity, lust, and evil desires. Don't be greedy, for a greedy person is an idolater, worshiping the things of this world. Because of these sins, the anger of God is coming. You used to do these things when your life was still part of this world. But now is the time to get rid of anger, rage, malicious behavior, slander, and dirty language. Don't lie to each other, for you have stripped off your old sinful nature and all its wicked deeds. Put on your new nature, and be renewed as you learn to know your Creator and become like Him."

We must understand spiritual maturity in order to see its value and make it an absolute priority. Most everyone understands the

19

importance of being saved, and it becomes a priority to many, but there is much more to "being saved." God intended for us to become disciples (followers) of Christ, and this will lead to true spiritual maturity.

Spiritual maturity is not you growing up, but Christ growing up in you. It is the process of you dying to self so that Christ's life may be manifest through you. "Oh, my dear children! I feel as if I'm going through labor pains for you again, and they will continue until Christ is fully developed in your lives" (Gal 4:19 NLT). Now these are the gifts Christ gave to the church: the apostles, the prophets, the evangelists, and the pastors and teachers. Their responsibility is to equip God's people to do his work and build up the church, the body of Christ. This will continue until we all come to such unity in our faith and knowledge of God's Son that we will be mature in the Lord, measuring up to the full and complete standard of Christ. Then we will no longer be immature like children. We won't be tossed and blown about by every wind of new teaching. We will not be influenced when people try to trick us with lies so clever they sound like the truth. Instead, we will speak the truth in love, growing in every way more and more like Christ, who is the head of his body, the church. (Eph 4:11-15 NLT).

You can see in the Scriptures that the gifts of the apostles, prophets, evangelists, pastors, and teachers are for our spiritual maturity. If we are not faithful in attending church and allowing the gifts from God to speak into our lives, we will never actually be able to grow up spiritually. We can now see how church attendance and listening to and following solid biblical teaching is essential for our spiritual maturity.

Another essential component to spiritual maturity is continuing fellowship with the Body of Christ. Daily interaction and involvement with the church, which the Scriptures call the Body of Christ, is highly important. God relates His body to a physical body; just as each member of the body needs and depends on the other, so we depend on each member of the Body of Christ. We must be connected so that we are receiving what they give for our continued spiritual growth and maturity. Others depend on us as well, so our life is valuable to others just as theirs is valuable to us. "From Him the whole body, joined and held together by every supporting ligament, grows and builds itself up in love, as each part does its work" (Eph 4:16 NIV).

> Just as our bodies have many parts and each part has a special function, so it is with Christ's body. We are many parts of one body, and we all belong to each other.
>
> In His grace, God has given us different gifts for doing certain things well. So if God has given you the ability to prophesy, speak out with as much faith as God has given you. If your gift is serving others, serve them well. If you are a teacher, teach well. If your gift is to encourage others, be encouraging. If it is giving, give generously. If God has given you leadership ability, take the responsibility seriously. And if you have a gift for showing kindness to others, do it gladly.
>
> Don't just pretend to love others. Really love them. Hate what is wrong. Hold tightly to what is good. Love each other with genuine affection, and take delight in honoring each other. Never be lazy, but work hard and serve the Lord enthusiastically. Rejoice in our confident hope. Be patient in trouble, and keep on praying. When God's people are in need, be ready to help them. Always be eager to practice hospitality. (Rom 12:4-13 NLT)

As you can see from the Scriptures, our involvement with the church is critical and should never be neglected. It not only affects our spiritual maturity but also affects others' spiritual maturity. Slacking in church attendance and involvement will inevitably lead to regression in your spiritual maturity and ultimately result in you backsliding from the person God is forming you to be.

Hebrews 10:23-31 (NLT) instructs:

> Let us hold tightly without wavering to the hope we affirm, for God can be trusted to keep His promise. Let us think of ways to motivate one another to acts of love and good works. And let us not neglect our meeting together, as some people do, but encourage one another, especially now that the day of His return is drawing near.
>
> Dear friends, if we deliberately continue sinning after we have received knowledge of the truth, there is no longer any

sacrifice that will cover these sins. There is only the terrible expectation of God's judgment and the raging fire that will consume His enemies. For anyone who refused to obey the law of Moses was put to death without mercy on the testimony of two or three witnesses. Just think how much worse the punishment will be for those who have trampled on the Son of God, and have treated the blood of the covenant, which made us holy, as if it were common and unholy, and have insulted and disdained the Holy Spirit who brings God's mercy to us. For we know the one who said,

"I will take revenge. I will pay them back."
He also said,
"The LORD will judge His own people."
It is a terrible thing to fall into the hands of the living God.

Too often, we hear people say you don't have to go to church to get to heaven in an attempt to justify not attending. The fact is, based on Scripture and not opinion, attending church is essential to fulfilling God's will and spiritual maturity, which results in a life free from addiction.

# CHAPTER 6

## Developing Your Prayer Life

Prayer is another essential key to spiritual maturity and living a life that is free from addiction. To understand prayer fully, you must realize prayer is not a one-sided conversation where we talk to God. It is also a time when we position ourselves for God to speak to us. Prayer is our gift of communication with God and not just a "give me" session where I tell God what I need and want. Any relationship must have clear communication; we have a relationship with God, and for that relationship to grow it must involve communication. God already knows more about us than we know about ourselves so, therefore, our prayer to God must be transparent and from our heart. We do not need to take on a religious posture and pray prayers we think are religiously correct but instead be ourselves and share our heart with God about everything.

Matthew 6:5-8 (NLT) cautions us:

"When you pray, don't be like the hypocrites who love to pray publicly on street corners and in the synagogues where everyone can see them. I tell you the truth, that is all the reward they will ever get. But when you pray, go away by yourself, shut the door behind you, and pray to your Father in private. Then your Father, who sees everything, will reward you.

"When you pray, don't babble on and on as people of other religions do. They think their prayers are answered merely by repeating their words again and again. Don't be like them, for your Father knows exactly what you need even before you ask him!"

God cares about every detail of our life and wants to communicate with us about those details. If God cares enough about us to have every single hair on our head numbered, He cares about what is going on in our lives. Let me share the real meaning of when He says He has the hairs of our head numbered. This means He knows when number 1,297 comes out of your head and goes down the drain while you are showering. If God is that concerned about the details of your hairs, then He certainly cares about everything else. You are valuable to God, and He is interested in hearing from you. "What is the price of five sparrows—two copper coins? Yet God does not forget a single one of them. And the very hairs on your head are all numbered. So don't be afraid; you are more valuable to God than a whole flock of sparrows" (Lk 12:6-7 NLT).

Jesus instructs us in how we should develop our prayer life. This pattern lays the foundation for clear and honest communication with God. Below is what Jesus taught about prayer, and I will further expound on it, giving you clear understanding of this lesson Jesus taught.

> After this manner therefore pray ye: Our Father which art in heaven, Hallowed be Thy name.
> Thy kingdom come. Thy will be done in earth, as it is in heaven.
> Give us this day our daily bread.
> And forgive us our debts, as we forgive our debtors.
> And lead us not into temptation, but deliver us from evil: For Thine is the kingdom, and the power, and the glory, for ever. Amen.
> For if ye forgive men their trespasses, your heavenly Father will also forgive you:
> But if ye forgive not men their trespasses, neither will your Father forgive your trespasses. (Mt 6:9-15 KJV)

The Lord's Prayer:

1. The prayer begins by understanding our relationship with God, "Our Father." God is our Father, and we are His sons and daughters, and He loves us and longs for time and communication with us. Our prayers must be filled with faith and belief, or they are powerless. You must understand that God does hear you, and He wants and desires to hear from you. If you think for a moment that God does not want to hear from you or that He views you as something less than a son or daughter, your approach will be with doubt and fear. You may even feel like prayer is pointless and unnecessary if He doesn't want to hear from you or won't listen to you. Once again, God loves you as

His children and He does want to hear from you because you are His family.

2. You must acknowledge and understand God's position, "Which art in Heaven."

   □ His OMNIPRESENCE. "The heaven and heaven of heavens cannot contain Thee" (1 Kgs 8:27 KJV). That is, Thou fillest immensity.

   □ His MAJESTY and DOMINION over His creatures. "Art not Thou God in heaven, and rulest not Thou over all the kingdoms of the heathen?" (2 Chr 20:6 KJV).

   □ His POWER and MIGHT. "And in Thine hand is there not power and might, so that none is able to withstand Thee?" (2 Chr 20:6 KJV). "Our God is in heaven, and hath done whatsoever He pleased" (Ps 115:3 KJV).

   □ His OMNISCIENCE. "The Lord's throne is in heaven: His eyes behold, His eyelids try, the children of men" (Ps 11:4 KJV). "The Lord looketh from heaven, He beholdeth all the sons of men" (Ps 33:13-15 KJV).

   □ His infinite PURITY and HOLINESS. "The high and lofty One, who inhabiteth eternity, whose name is holy" (Is 57:15 KJV).

3. You must recognize His Holiness: "Hallowed be Thy Name." God is a holy God, and we dare not approach a holy God with insincerity and without reverence for who He is. He is HOLY. The truth is that we could never approach God except through the Blood of Jesus that has washed us from our sins.

   We would have no access to even talk to God if not for what He provided through the death and resurrection of Jesus. We can now see what a WONDERFUL GIFT prayer is. Prayer is an honor and a privilege that was given to us by God; it came at the most expensive price heaven could give, the life of Jesus His Son. Therefore, we should value the opportunity God has given us and approach God with great gratitude.

4. To pray effectively, you must position yourself under the Lordship of Jesus, "Thy Kingdom Come, Thy Will be Done on Earth as it is in Heaven." When most people think of the Kingdom of Heaven or the Kingdom of God, they think of an eternal place beyond the clouds called heaven. This is not the case, and it is not what the Scripture is talking about or referring to.

The Kingdom is referring to the King and His reign as Lord over His Kingdom. The Scriptures tell us that the Kingdom of God is within us. "Once, having been asked by the Pharisees when the kingdom of God would come, Jesus replied, 'The coming of the kingdom of God is not something that can be observed, nor will people say, 'Here it is,' or 'There it is,' because the kingdom of God is within you'" (Lk 17:20-21 NIV).

The Kingdom of God is within every person who has surrendered his life to the Lordship of Jesus, meaning He reigns in his life. This is why Jesus tells us in Matthew 7:21 that not everyone who calls Him "Lord, Lord" will enter the Kingdom of Heaven but only those who do the will of the Father. When we pray "thy Kingdom come thy will be done," we are saying we surrender ourselves to the will of God in everything. We are asking for God's will to be done on earth as it is in heaven, so we are acknowledging that we are His vessels submitted to His Lordship to carry out His will on earth just like His will is carried out in Heaven by the heavenly angels and beings.

There is only one account of rebellion in heaven and that was Lucifer the devil, and he and all his followers were cast out of heaven because God does not allow rebellion in heaven. If He does not allow it in heaven, then why would He allow it in us? When we do not yield our lives to His Lordship, then His will is not carried out in the earth. This shows that our lives are very valuable to God and His plan is bigger than us, yet He chose to use us for His purpose on the earth. Your life has great worth and value when submitted to His Lordship. Prayer becomes effective when it is prayed from a person who is fully submitted to the will of God.

"This is the confidence we have in approaching God: that if we ask anything according to His will, He hears us. And if we know that He hears us—whatever we ask—we know that we have what we asked of Him" (1 Jn 5:14-15 NIV).

God further teaches us if we seek His will and surrender to it, He will make clear the path and direction. He has prepared for all aspects of our life. "Trust in the LORD with all your heart; do not depend on your own understanding. Seek His will in all you do, and He will show you which path to take" (Prv 3:5-6 NLT).

5. Effective praying includes asking for daily provision, and it must always follow full submission to God's will. After teaching about His will being done on earth as it is heaven, He said pray for your daily bread. Bread represents the daily necessities of life, which God desires to provide for His children. Provision always follows submission to God's will.

According to Matthew 6:28-33 (NLT), "And why worry about your clothing? Look at the lilies of the field and how they grow. They don't work or make their clothing, yet Solomon in all his glory was not dressed as beautifully as they are. And if God cares so wonderfully for wildflowers that are here today and thrown into the fire tomorrow, He will certainly care for you. Why do you have so little faith? So don't worry about these things, saying, 'What will we eat? What will we drink? What will we wear?' These things dominate the thoughts of unbelievers, but your heavenly Father already knows all your needs. Seek the Kingdom of God above all else, and live righteously, and He will give you everything you need."

God truly longs to provide for His sons and daughters firstly because He loves us; secondly it is in the nature of who He is. One of the names of God in the Old Testament is Jehovah-Jireh, translating in the Hebrew as "God my Provider." In Scripture, a name denotes the character of a person, and it is in the character of God to provide for His children.

"The LORD directs the steps of the godly. He delights in every detail of their lives. Though they stumble, they will never fall, for the LORD holds them by the hand. Once I was young, and now I am old. Yet I have never seen the godly abandoned or their children begging for bread. The godly always give generous loans to others, and their children are a blessing. Turn from evil and do good, and you will live in the land forever" (Ps 37:23-27 NLT).

We learn more from Philippians 4:18-20 (NLT): "At the moment I have all I need—and more! I am generously supplied with the gifts you sent me with Epaphroditus. They are a sweet-smelling sacrifice that is acceptable and pleasing to God. And this same God who takes care of me will supply all your needs from His glorious riches, which have been given to us in Christ Jesus. Now all glory to God our Father forever and ever! Amen."

It is important to ask God for our daily needs because our focus and attention on His will can become distracted by worry and fear. This can lead to spiritual decline and relapse.

6. Six steps into Jesus teaching us about prayer, He teaches us to ask for forgiveness of our sins (disobedience to God). Most Christians tend to focus on forgiveness first—thinking God will not listen to us or be angry with us because we sin, yet Jesus puts the request toward the end of the prayer. Actually, He lists it after provision. This is not because our sin is not important, but that there are other things that will affect the sincerity of our repentance and request for forgiveness. Praise and exaltation of God puts us in the awareness of His presence. A desire to be submissive to His will is actually the act of repentance and shows our heart is genuinely remorseful for our sin. Asking for forgiveness without a change is simply words.

"This then is the message which we have heard of Him, and declare unto you, that God is light, and in Him is no darkness at all. If we say that we have fellowship with Him, and walk in darkness, we lie, and do not the truth: But if we walk in the light, as He is in the light, we have fellowship one with another, and the blood of Jesus Christ His Son cleanseth us from all sin" (1 Jn 1:5-7 KJV).

As you can see from this verse, as we put ourselves in the light as He is in the light, the blood of Jesus cleanses us.

Another important thing Jesus teaches about asking Him to forgive us is that we must forgive those who have sinned against us because our forgiveness is contingent upon us forgiving others.

"For if ye forgive men their trespasses, your heavenly Father will also forgive you: But if ye forgive not men their trespasses, neither will your Father forgive your trespasses" (Mt 6:14-15).

7. Asking God to lead and order our steps is an important part of our prayer life. As we have seen, submitting to His will at all times in all things becomes the key to not being led into temptation. Temptation is more than just being tempted by a sin, but it also refers to trials. I believe Jesus is telling us to ask to be led into paths that do not require unnecessary temptation and trials. We must look at a few Scriptures to gain full understanding of this portion of prayer. God never tempts any man, but temptation comes from the flesh and Satan.

"And remember, when you are being tempted, do not say, 'God is tempting me.' God is never tempted to do wrong, and He never tempts anyone else. Temptation comes from our own desires, which entice us and drag us away. These desires give birth to sinful actions. And when sin is allowed to grow, it gives birth to death. So don't be misled, my dear brothers and sisters. Whatever is good and perfect is a gift coming down to us from God our Father, who created all the lights in the heavens. He never changes or casts a shifting shadow. He chose to give birth to us by giving us His true word. And we, out of all creation, became His prized possession" (Jas 1:13-18 NLT).

Our purpose and heart should always be to bring glory and honor to God and His name so when we live triumphantly over temptation of sin and triumph over trials, we honor and glorify God. Living for God does not exempt us from temptations and trials, but it does mean God is working on our behalf to give us victory and even working in our lives to help prevent us from being in unnecessary situations. Because men are evil and not all walk according to His will, this means that there are times when we will face unjust temptations and trials, but God is with us.

"If you think you are standing strong, be careful not to fall. The temptations in your life are no different from what others experience. And God is faithful. He will not allow the temptation to be more than you can stand. When you are tempted, He will show you a way out so that you can endure" (1 Cor 10:12-13 NLT).

To sum up this portion of prayer we could say that asking God not to lead us into temptation but deliver us from evil is to ask God not to allow us to walk in a path that leads to unnecessary temptation and trial, but if we find ourselves there, deliver us from the evil intended so we may glorify and honor His Name with our lives and actions.

There is another lesson from the Scriptures that will help us to have an effective prayer life and keep us walking free from addiction. When we face troubles, we should not simply pray a knee-jerk reaction prayer or pray what we want or think is best. We must pray and seek God with confidence and trust that He hears us and will respond. It is okay if we don't know what to pray; we should inquire of the Lord for wisdom and direction. When David and his mighty men's families were taken by the Amalekites, David was in great pain and distress, but the Scripture declares that he encouraged himself in the Lord and enquired of the Lord what he should do (1 Sm 30).

James shares this same truth that is so important as it relates to effective prayer. "Dear brothers and sisters, when troubles of any kind come your way, consider it an opportunity for great joy. For you know that when your faith is tested, your endurance has a chance to grow. So let it grow, for when your endurance is fully developed, you will be perfect and complete, needing nothing. If you need wisdom, ask our generous God, and He will give it to you. He will not rebuke you for asking. But when you ask Him, be sure that your faith is in God alone. Do not waver, for a person with divided loyalty is as unsettled as a wave of the sea that is blown and tossed by the wind. Such people should not expect to receive anything from the Lord. Their loyalty is divided between God and the world, and they are unstable in everything they do" (Jas 1:2-8 NLT).

# CHAPTER 7

## Right Relationships for Righteous Living

Choosing the people you allow in your life is another key to becoming the person God has created you to be and living a life free from addiction. Peer pressure has always been one of the most effective weapons Satan uses against us. Past, present, and future relationships can be a huge stumbling block in your pursuit of God and in your journey of obedience to His will.

According to 2 Corinthians 6:14-18 (NIV),

Do not be yoked together with unbelievers. For what do righteousness and wickedness have in common? Or what fellowship can light have with darkness? What harmony is there between Christ and Belial? What does a believer have in common with an unbeliever? What agreement is there between the temple of God and idols? For we are the temple of the living God. As God has said:

"I will live with them
and walk among them,
and I will be their God,
and they will be My people."

Therefore,

"Come out from them
and be separate,
says the Lord.
Touch no unclean thing,
and I will receive you."

And,

"I will be a Father to you,
and you will be My sons and daughters,
says the Lord Almighty."

To move forward in your spiritual maturity and develop your new life means that you may very well have to let go of old relationships with

31

people that still live a lifestyle you once lived. If you are truly following Christ, you will find you have nothing in common with them, and relationships are usually based on things you share in common. Letting go of past relationships is not usually a one-sided thing that is all on you. In fact, if you are truly allowing Christ, the new man, to manifest through you then you will find that those old friends will, in most cases, draw back from you. This is actually scriptural and should be normal for a person living a devoted life to Christ because you have become the light of Christ. Remember, light and darkness have nothing in common.

> "Don't participate in the things these people do. For once you were full of darkness, but now you have light from the Lord. So live as people of light! For this light within you produces only what is good and right and true.
> Carefully determine what pleases the Lord. Take no part in the worthless deeds of evil and darkness; instead, expose them. It is shameful even to talk about the things that ungodly people do in secret. But their evil intentions will be exposed when the light shines on them, for the light makes everything visible. This is why it is said,
> "Awake, O sleeper,
> rise up from the dead,
> and Christ will give you light." (Eph 5:7-14 NLT)

"And the judgment is based on this fact: God's light came into the world, but people loved the darkness more than the light, for their actions were evil. All who do evil hate the light and refuse to go near it for fear their sins will be exposed. But those who do what is right come to the light so others can see that they are doing what God wants" (Jn 3:19-21 NLT).

How old acquaintances and friends respond to you can be a reflection of how you are actually living and which life you are allowing to shine through you. If old friends are comfortable around you, then you may not be as spiritually strong as you think you are. Because you are now the light of the Lord, you will more than likely make your old acquaintances feel extremely uncomfortable, and this is normal.

"If the world hates you, remember that it hated Me first. The world would love you as one of its own if you belonged to it, but you are no longer part of the world. I chose you to come out of the world, so it hates you. Do you remember what I told you? 'A slave is not greater than the master.' Since they persecuted Me, naturally they will persecute you. And if they had listened to Me, they would listen to you" (Jn 15:18-20 NLT).

Choosing new and present relationships are very important and should be done with care and caution. Not everyone who attends church or says they are a Christian are actually what they say they are. Perhaps they may not be strong enough in their faith to have a positive influence in your life. The Scriptures tell us we will know a tree by the fruit it bears, and we should always examine the lifestyle and behavior of a person to make sure he/she has the fruit that would be beneficial for our life. The word of God teaches us to do so and clearly defines that a person's lifestyle is a means to know if he/she is truly a follower of Christ.

"So now we can tell who are children of God and who are children of the devil. Anyone who does not live righteously and does not love other believers does not belong to God" (1 Jn 3:10 NLT).

If you choose to enter a relationship with a person who is religious but doesn't live godly, it can very well lead you down a path of destruction and even back to the old lifestyle of addiction God has delivered you from.

Jesus tells us in Luke 6:39-45 (NLT):

Then Jesus gave the following illustration: "Can one blind person lead another? Won't they both fall into a ditch? Students are not greater than their teacher. But the student who is fully trained will become like the teacher.

"And why worry about a speck in your friend's eye when you have a log in your own? How can you think of saying, 'Friend, let me help you get rid of that speck in your eye,' when you can't see past the log in your own eye? Hypocrite! First get rid of the log in your own eye; then you will see well enough to deal with the speck in your friend's eye.

"A good tree can't produce bad fruit, and a bad tree can't produce good fruit. A tree is identified by its fruit. Figs never grow on thornbushes, nor grapes on bramble bushes. A good person produces good things from the treasury of a good heart, and an evil person produces evil things from the treasury of an evil heart. What you say flows from what is in your heart."

Make sure the people you choose as friends are spiritually mature so they will be able to help you if you stray from your obedience to God. If they themselves are not mature in Christ, they will not be able to help you and the relationship could be detrimental to the both of you.

"Dear brothers and sisters, if another believer is overcome by some sin, you who are godly should gently and humbly help that person back onto the right path. And be careful not to fall into the same temptation yourself" (Gal 6:1 NLT).

A true friend will always tell you the truth, encourage you, edify you, correct you, and forgive you. Beware of a relationship where people tell you what you want to hear for the sake of the relationship.

"An open rebuke is better than hidden love! Wounds from a sincere friend are better than many kisses from an enemy" (Prv 27:5-6 NLT).

Relationships of all kinds are something that you have control over; they do not simply happen. You have the ability to choose your friends, so choose people who will be a help to you and encourage your spiritual growth. You can do this by being friendly yourself.

"A man who has friends must himself be friendly, But there is a friend who sticks closer than a brother" (Prv 18:24 NKJV).

Once you have begun to mature and have grown stable in your walk with God, it is important to have two types of friendships. Relationships with people who are helping you in your walk with God and relationships with people you can help in their walk with God. We all need to be disciples, and we also need to disciple others once we are mature enough.

"You have been believers so long now that you ought to be teaching others. Instead, you need someone to teach you again the basic things about God's word. You are like babies who need milk and cannot eat solid food. For someone who lives on milk is still an infant and doesn't know how to do what is right. Solid food is for those who are mature, who through training have the skill to recognize the difference between right and wrong" (Heb 5:12-14 NLT).

You may ask the question, "What about my lost friends? Shouldn't I witness to them?" The answer is yes, but you must first be mature enough to do so and strong enough in your faith that you do not allow yourself to be led astray by those you are witnessing to. Attempting to do this can be a danger to you and the one you are ministering to. When we witness to others and then have them see us fall, it harms your testimony and the testimony of God, so it is vitally important that you are grounded in the Lord before attempting to win your lost friends.

"And now, just as you accepted Christ Jesus as your Lord, you must continue to follow Him. Let your roots grow down into Him, and let your lives be built on Him. Then your faith will grow strong in the truth you were taught, and you will overflow with thankfulness" (Col 2:6-7 NLT).

# CHAPTER 8

## Taking Off the Mask

Transparency with God and ourselves is one of the most important keys to living a life free of addiction and is a must for healing of family and broken relationships.

"The human heart is the most deceitful of all things, and desperately wicked. Who really knows how bad it is? But I, the LORD, search all hearts and examine secret motives. I give all people their due rewards, according to what their actions deserve" (Jer 17:9-10 NLT).

God knows more about us than we actually know about ourselves because He sees beyond our own self-deception, pride, and misunderstandings. When addiction has controlled someone's life, actions, and decisions for long periods of time, a person develops a lifestyle of lies and manipulation to justify the addiction. They become part of the person's identity, character, and daily behavior. In most cases, one can live this lifestyle for so long that one actually believes the lies one tells others and believes the lies one tells themselves, seeing absolutely no wrong in what one is doing. This is just another way that addiction controls an individual's life and maintains that control. This behavior is not easily or quickly changed, but it can be done by the grace of God and obedience to His word.

The first step to being free from addiction is knowing the truth. Truth is more than the Scriptures, although they are truth. An example of a truth would be that I am a 50-year-old Caucasian male. It does not matter if you don't believe me; it is the truth. No matter how much it is denied, it is still the truth. If you tell a person a truth about himself/herself that is actually a truth, then it is truth no matter if that person does not see it or believe it. When I was an addict with a $250-a-day cocaine habit, people tried to tell me I had a problem, but I would argue and tell them I did not. However, the truth is that I did have a problem. When I saw the truth for myself—that I was an alcoholic and a drug addict—then I could change. But only then.

Only when we can hear and embrace the truth about ourselves and our actions can we begin the journey of transformation and change.

Jesus gave a powerful teaching on the truth and how it sets us free from the slavery of sin, and that is exactly what an addiction is—sin.

We learn from John 8:31-36 (NLT):

> Jesus said to the people who believed in Him, "You are truly My disciples if you remain faithful to My teachings. And you will know the truth, and the truth will set you free."
>
> "But we are descendants of Abraham," they said. "We have never been slaves to anyone. What do You mean, 'You will be set free'?"
>
> Jesus replied, "I tell you the truth, everyone who sins is a slave of sin. A slave is not a permanent member of the family, but a son is part of the family forever. So if the Son sets you free, you are truly free.

We learn from 2 Corinthians 3:18 that God's word is truth and like a mirror reflecting who we should be and what we should like. Everything that is not what the mirror of God's word reflects must be removed. God's word will examine us if we keep it and show us things about ourselves that need to be repented of and removed from our lives. God also uses godly people to show truths about us that will reveal what needs to be changed. God places people in our lives to expose the truth about us so we can be changed.

"For once you were full of darkness, but now you have light from the Lord. So live as people of light! For this light within you produces only what is good and right and true. Carefully determine what pleases the Lord. Take no part in the worthless deeds of evil and darkness; instead, expose them. It is shameful even to talk about the things that ungodly people do in secret. But their evil intentions will be exposed when the light shines on them" (Eph 5:8-13 NLT).

If we are not open to the truth and willing to allow God to manifest truth as it relates to our life and behavior, it makes it impossible for us to be changed. David cried to the Lord for Him to search his heart and that should be the desire of those who have repented and chosen to follow Christ.

"Search me, O God, and know my heart; test me and know my anxious thoughts. Point out anything in me that offends You, and lead me along the path of everlasting life" (Ps 139:23-24 NLT).

David wanted God to search him through and through and reveal to him what wasn't right and then lead him in the path of everlasting life. David also asked the Lord to create in him a clean heart after he had failed with Bathsheba. David understood that he was capable of lying to himself and believing his own lies. He also understood that it would take God to create a clean heart within him that is not deceitful and dark.

"Create in me a clean heart, O God. Renew a loyal spirit within me" (Ps 51:10 NLT).

To take off the mask and become transparent, one must be open to the truth and willing to embrace it. For that to happen you must be willing to open yourself up and desire for God to search out your heart with His word and by people. It was the prophet Nathan who exposed David's heart. I have met many people, including myself, who have said, "God knows my heart." Yes, He does, but that does not mean that we are willing to accept what He knows about us. We cannot be afraid to hear the truth from others who love us or from the word of God. Many times, we say to those God tries to use to reveal truth about us, "Don't judge me," but the truth has already judged you; you must desire for truth to judge you so you can be honest with God and be changed. Honesty is a must. When honesty is not there, manipulation begins and has free reign in our lives. The defenses we use when confronted with truth are simply manipulation at work to prevent us from hearing the truth. How many people have we manipulated to get what we want and to avoid having to be confronted with truth? If you can be honest, it will be more than you can count. This lifestyle destroys trust and respect that people who love you once had for you. Family and friends may still love you but have no respect or trust in you. This should not be an excuse for you to be angry and bitter at anyone, but instead this truth should be a catalyst for you to change.

The first step to regaining trust and respect is for them to see you being honest and transparent. For others to see your honesty and transparency, you must be that way with yourself and God first. Once you are able, by the grace of God, to be honest and transparent with yourself and with God, you will have no problem being that way with others. In time, they will see it. It is often forgotten how long you lived a lie and manipulated friends and loved ones. It took years for most people to destroy the trust and respect they once had for you. You cannot expect them to give it back just because you say you have changed. In most cases that is not how it can happen. It will take time for you to regain trust and respect through living and exemplifying a lifestyle of honesty and transparency that proves you have become a new person deserving of that trust and respect.

Coming from a lifestyle of addiction, and being free now for over twenty-seven years, I can remember the damage I did to myself and my family through lies and manipulation. I never told the truth about anything as it related to my addiction or lifestyle. I was never honest and was always manipulating those I loved to cover up what I was and what I was doing. This behavior destroyed everything of value in my life. Once I became honest with myself and God began this amazing transformation in my life, it took three or four years for trust and respect to be regained. I never became angry about this because I was the one who destroyed it in the first place, and no one owed me anything because of what I had done. As I walked daily in an open and honest relationship with God and myself, the change became evident and those who were once disappointed and ashamed of me became those who trusted and respected me most. One of the greatest honors I have had in my life is to be a pastor to my family. Those who know me best—the good, the bad, and the ugly—trust and respect me with the honor of being their pastor and spiritual leader. This testimony is to show you that God can change and restore anything if you allow Him to, but it is going to require you to take off the mask, open your heart to the truth, embrace it, and walk in it.

# CHAPTER 9

## Your Identity in Christ

Coming to an understanding of who God has created you to be, who you are in Him, as well as seeing yourself as He sees you, are significant keys to walking in freedom from addiction and reaching the full potential God has given you. Let's start with who and what God has created you to be.

You must understand that God created you, and He never makes junk. You are His masterpiece regardless of how you see yourself or how others see you. You may appear to be flawed and useless, but that is not how God has created you.

> You made all the delicate, inner parts of my body
>> and knit me together in my mother's womb.
> Thank You for making me so wonderfully complex!
>> Your workmanship is marvelous—how well I know it.
>
> You watched me as I was being formed in utter seclusion,
>> as I was woven together in the dark of the womb.
> You saw me before I was born.
>> Every day of my life was recorded in Your book.
> Every moment was laid out
>> before a single day had passed.
> How precious are Your thoughts about me, O God.
>> They cannot be numbered!
> I can't even count them;
>> they outnumber the grains of sand!
> And when I wake up,
>> You are still with me! (Ps 139:13-18 NLT)

We are, according to Scripture, wonderfully made and a masterpiece to Him. Our lives are valuable to God, and He is at work in our lives every day, even when we were not living for Him. You may

41

ask, "Why am I so valuable to God?" It is because He created you in His very own image and likeness.

In Genesis 1:26-27 (NLT), "God said, 'Let Us make human beings in Our image, to be like Us. They will reign over the fish in the sea, the birds in the sky, the livestock, all the wild animals on the earth, and the small animals that scurry along the ground.' So God created human beings in His own image. In the image of God He created them; male and female He created them."

So God has created you to be in His image and in His likeness. You were created to be a reflection of Him, and this is why you are of such great value to Him. We will discuss the latter in this chapter. This has always been the plan of God for mankind, but sin entered the world and that image became marred due to Adam and Eve's sin. However, it did not affect God's plan because He sent His son Jesus to restore what Adam lost in the garden.

"Yes, Adam's one sin brings condemnation for everyone, but Christ's one act of righteousness brings a right relationship with God and new life for everyone. Because one person disobeyed God, many became sinners. But because one other person obeyed God, many will be made righteous" (Rom 5:18-19).

God has restored what was lost so that God's predestined plan for us would come to pass and His will and purpose could be carried out on earth and provide for us the eternal reward of everlasting life.

> And we know that God causes everything to work together for the good of those who love God and are called according to His purpose for them. For God knew His people in advance, and He chose them to become like His Son, so that His Son would be the firstborn among many brothers and sisters. And having chosen them, He called them to come to Him. And having called them, He gave them right standing with Himself. And having given them right standing, He gave them His glory. What shall we say about such wonderful things as these? If God is for us, who can ever be against us? Since He did not spare even His own Son but gave Him up for us all, won't He also give us everything else? Who dares accuse us whom God has chosen for His own? No one—for God Himself has given us right standing with Himself. (Rom 8:28-33 NLT)

Jesus is God incarnate in the flesh and is the manifestation of the very person of God.

"Who being the brightness of His glory, and the express image of His person, and upholding all things by the word of His power, when He had by Himself purged our sins, sat down on the right hand of the Majesty on high. So now we see that God has restored His image in us through what Jesus has done for us through His death and resurrection. What remains is us allowing God to work in us until that image is manifest in and through us" (Heb 1:3 KJV).

"But whenever someone turns to the Lord, the veil is taken away. For the Lord is the Spirit, and wherever the Spirit of the Lord is, there is freedom. So all of us who have had that veil removed can see and reflect the glory of the Lord. And the Lord—who is the Spirit—makes us more and more like Him as we are changed into His glorious image" (2 Cor 3:16-18 NLT).

To become that person who is a reflection of God we must see and understand who He is. We cannot become like someone we do not know or understand. This is why it is so important that we remain in constant fellowship and relationship with Him because through that relationship and fellowship we see what we are created to be and this is the only way to know and understand our identity. Paul illustrates this in a prayer he prayed for the Ephesian believers.

> Wherefore I also, after I heard of your faith in the Lord Jesus, and love unto all the saints,
> Cease not to give thanks for you, making mention of you in my prayers;
> That the God of our Lord Jesus Christ, the Father of glory, may give unto you the spirit of wisdom and revelation in the knowledge of Him:
> The eyes of your understanding being enlightened; that ye may know what is the hope of His calling, and what the riches of the glory of His inheritance in the saints,
> And what is the exceeding greatness of His power to us-ward who believe, according to the working of His mighty power,

Which He wrought in Christ, when He raised Him from the dead, and set Him at his own right hand in the heavenly places,

Far above all principality, and power, and might, and dominion, and every name that is named, not only in this world, but also in that which is to come:

And hath put all things under His feet, and gave Him to be the head over all things to the church,

Which is His body, the fullness of Him that filleth all in all. (Eph 1:15-23 KJV)

These few verses are filled with the keys that reveal what God's desires are for you to know so that you may manifest His life as the Body of Christ, which is the fullness of Him.

a. You need the spirit of wisdom and revelation in the knowledge of Him.

b. You need the eyes of your understanding enlightened so that you can know the hope of His calling and the inheritance He has placed within you (Himself). The calling is to become like Him.

c. You need to understand the power God has given to us to accomplish this calling and destiny to be His reflection.

d. You need to understand that there is no spiritual or physical power that can stop this calling except you refusing to allow God to have His will accomplished in your life.

e. You must understand that you are the physical part of His Body that He declares is the fullness of Him in the earth.

Now that we understand where our identity is from, we must also understand that the enemy does not want this to be accomplished in you because this means His defeat. The enemy will always try to create a false image of who you are, and he will use people to rob you by telling you that you are something different than what He has called you to be. You are not what your past says you are. You are who God says you are, so we must avoid allowing the identity of our past to define our present and future identity. The enemy has also provided a false image of God through religion. Many people end up becoming like a church or Christian organization of a denomination when, in fact, they look nothing like God. Just because they say they are a church and use the

44

name of Jesus does not mean they reflect the image of God. Be careful that you don't take on the image of religion; take on the image of God. Some people know far more about their church and its traditions than they do about God and His ways. It is possible to believe in an image of Jesus that is not Jesus at all, and this is the result of Satan using false teachers and preachers presenting a different Jesus that does not reflect who He is. This is why we must know Him personally and know Him by and through the Scriptures and not only by what we hear others say and profess about Him. If we receive an image that is not Him, we will pattern ourselves after this false image and lose our true identity.

"But I fear that somehow your pure and undivided devotion to Christ will be corrupted, just as Eve was deceived by the cunning ways of the serpent. You happily put up with whatever anyone tells you, even if they preach a different Jesus than the One we preach, or a different kind of Spirit than the One you received, or a different kind of gospel than the one you believed" (2 Cor 11:3-4 NLT).

Our identity is the key to understanding our purpose and its importance. Knowing our purpose and its significance to God gives our life meaning and becomes a key for us to live free from addictions. Our purpose and destiny are so important and fulfilling that it becomes another reason for us not to miss it or compromise it by yielding to the temptation of an addiction. If Adam and Eve would have understood their identity and purpose, they would not have listened to the serpent. One of his enticements was that they would be like God if they ate the fruit when in fact they were already like God. God had given them dominion over the earth and all that was in it so that they could bring forth His will by His authority, power, and provision. He gave them the purpose to populate the earth and be fruitful, but they lost their position and purpose.

Genesis 3:4-5 (NLT) tells us about the first temptation: "You won't die!" the serpent replied to the woman. "God knows that your eyes will be opened as soon as you eat it, and you will be like God, knowing both good and evil."

"So the LORD God banished them from the Garden of Eden, and He sent Adam out to cultivate the ground from which he had been made. After sending them out, the LORD God stationed a mighty cherubim to the east of the Garden of Eden. And He placed a flaming sword that flashed back and forth to guard the way to the tree of life" (Gen 3:23-24 NLT).

God has given you the purpose of manifesting His life on the earth, bringing His dominion, authority, and will to the earth through your obedience to Him and His will. He has also given you the purpose of populating the earth and being fruitful, not with just natural children but by sowing the seed of Christ and bringing people into the Kingdom of God through being born-again. When we bear the fruit of the Holy Spirit (nature of God) then others partake of that fruit and the seed is in the fruit. Let me give you several Scripture references for more understanding.

"But if you remain in Me and My words remain in you, you may ask for anything you want, and it will be granted! When you produce much fruit, you are My true disciples. This brings great glory to My Father" (Jn 15:7-23 NLT).

Furthermore in John 17:14-23 (NLT) we learn, "I have given them Your word. And the world hates them because they do not belong to the world, just as I do not belong to the world. I'm not asking You to take them out of the world, but to keep them safe from the evil one. They do not belong to this world any more than I do. Make them holy by Your truth; teach them Your word, which is truth. Just as You sent Me into the world, I am sending them into the world. And I give Myself as a holy sacrifice for them so they can be made holy by Your truth. I am praying not only for these disciples but also for all who will ever believe in Me through their message. I pray that they will all be one, just as You and I are one—as You are in Me, Father, and I am in You. And may they be in Us so that the world will believe You sent Me. I have given them the glory You gave Me, so they may be one as We are one. I am in them and You are in Me. May they experience such perfect unity that the world will know that You sent Me and that You love them as much as You love Me."

Matthew 5:14-16 (NLT) puts it this way: "You are the light of the world—like a city on a hilltop that cannot be hidden. No one lights a lamp and then puts it under a basket. Instead, a lamp is placed on a stand, where it gives light to everyone in the house. In the same way, let Your good deeds shine out for all to see, so that everyone will praise Your heavenly Father."

"[A]nd from Jesus Christ. He is the faithful witness to these things, the first to rise from the dead, and the ruler of all the kings of the world. All glory to Him who loves us and has freed us from our sins by shedding His blood for us. He has made us a Kingdom of priests for God His Father. All glory and power to Him forever and ever! Amen" (Rev 1:5-6 NLT).

"But you are not like that, for you are a chosen people. You are royal priests, a holy nation, God's very own possession. As a result, you can show others the goodness of God, for He called you out of the darkness into His wonderful light" (1 Pt 2:9 NLT).

As you can see, our lives have significant purpose and that purpose is to manifest God to the world through our obedience to Him. Therefore, our lives are significant to God and to others. If we fail to live our lives for Him and instead fulfill our own purpose, we don't just fail ourselves and God but we fail others who are counting on us to bring them the life of God.

> The human body has many parts, but the many parts make up one whole body. So it is with the body of Christ. Some of us are Jews, some are Gentiles, some are slaves, and some are free. But we have all been baptized into one body by one Spirit, and we all share the same Spirit.
>
> Yes, the body has many different parts, not just one part. If the foot says, "I am not a part of the body because I am not a hand," that does not make it any less a part of the body. And if the ear says, "I am not part of the body because I am not an eye," would that make it any less a part of the body? If the whole body were an eye, how would you hear? Or if your whole body were an ear, how would you smell anything?
>
> But our bodies have many parts, and God has put each part just where He wants it. How strange a body would be if it had only one part! Yes, there are many parts, but only one body. The eye can never say to the hand, "I don't need you." The head can't say to the feet, "I don't need you."
>
> In fact, some parts of the body that seem weakest and least important are actually the most necessary. And the parts we regard as less honorable are those we clothe with the greatest care. So we carefully protect those parts that should not be

47

seen, while the more honorable parts do not require this special care. So God has put the body together such that extra honor and care are given to those parts that have less dignity. This makes for harmony among the members, so that all the members care for each other. If one part suffers, all the parts suffer with it, and if one part is honored, all the parts are glad.

All of you together are Christ's body, and each of you is a part of it. (1 Cor 12:12-27 NLT)

# CHAPTER 10

## Deliverance and Spiritual Warfare

There is a lot to be taught and learned about these two subjects, and they go hand in hand. Deliverance and spiritual warfare are one of the keys to living a life of freedom from all addictions. Our God is a delivering God; He can and will deliver us from any and all forms of bondage. As we saw in earlier chapters, Satan is the author of sin, and it is his greatest weapon against you. We have also seen how sin has the power to make us slaves. Rest assured, Satan will do anything to entice you to become a slave to any sin. In most of your cases, that bondage has been drugs of all kinds, alcohol, and many other addictive substances. Bondages are not limited to these things but can include any sin such as sex, pornography, relationships, gambling, lying, hobbies, and even gossip just to name a few. They are all dangerous, and God can deliver us from them all. Let's look at how Satan is the author of sin and how his works have been destroyed through Jesus.

Satan has been sinning from the beginning, but Jesus was manifested for the purpose of destroying his works.

"He that committeth sin is of the devil; for the devil sinneth from the beginning. For this purpose the Son of God was manifested, that He might destroy the works of the devil" (1 Jn 3:8 KJV).

An example of how Satan uses sin is found in Genesis where he tempts Eve with sin that became a bondage and cost her everything.

The serpent was the shrewdest of all the wild animals the LORD God had made. One day he asked the woman, "Did God really say you must not eat the fruit from any of the trees in the garden?"

"Of course we may eat fruit from the trees in the garden," the woman replied.

"It's only the fruit from the tree in the middle of the garden that we are not allowed to eat. God said, 'You must not eat it or even touch it; if you do, you will die.'"

"You won't die!" the serpent replied to the woman. "God knows that your eyes will be opened as soon as you eat it, and you will be like God, knowing both good and evil."

The woman was convinced. She saw that the tree was beautiful and its fruit looked delicious, and she wanted the wisdom it would give her. So she took some of the fruit and ate it. Then she gave some to her husband, who was with her, and he ate it, too. (Gen 3:1-6 NLT)

Now that we see how Satan uses sin to bring us into bondage, let's look at how Jesus delivered us all from this incarcerating power. He first told us in the Scriptures what He had the power to do.

"The Spirit of the LORD is upon Me, for He has anointed Me to bring Good News to the poor. He has sent Me to proclaim that captives will be released, that the blind will see, that the oppressed will be set free, and that the time of the LORD's favor has come" (Lk 4:18-19 NLT).

We see this ministry was given to the Apostle Paul for the Gentiles. "Now get to your feet! For I have appeared to you to appoint you as My servant and witness. Tell people that you have seen Me, and tell them what I will show you in the future. And I will rescue you from both your own people and the Gentiles. Yes, I am sending you to the Gentiles to open their eyes, so they may turn from darkness to light and from the power of Satan to God. Then they will receive forgiveness for their sins and be given a place among God's people, who are set apart by faith in Me" (Acts 26:16-18 NLT).

Jesus set many people in the Scriptures free from their past bondages.

And the scribes and Pharisees brought unto Him a woman taken in adultery; and when they had set her in the midst,
They say unto Him, "Master, this woman was taken in adultery, in the very act.
Now Moses in the law commanded us, that such should be stoned: but what sayest thou?"
This they said, tempting Him, that they might have to accuse Him. But Jesus stooped down, and with His finger wrote on the ground, as though He heard them not.

So when they continued asking Him, He lifted up himself, and said unto them, "He that is without sin among you, let him first cast a stone at her."

And again He stooped down, and wrote on the ground.

And they which heard it, being convicted by their own conscience, went out one by one, beginning at the eldest, even unto the last: and Jesus was left alone, and the woman standing in the midst.

When Jesus had lifted up Himself, and saw none but the woman, He said unto her, "Woman, where are those thine accusers? hath no man condemned thee?"

She said, "No man, Lord." And Jesus said unto her, "Neither do I condemn thee: go, and sin no more." (Jn 8:3-11 KJV)

In John, chapter 4, we learn of when He set the woman at the well free from the bondage of broken and failed relationships. Likewise, He delivered Zacchaeus from thievery.

There was a man there named Zacchaeus. He was the chief tax collector in the region, and he had become very rich. He tried to get a look at Jesus, but he was too short to see over the crowd. So he ran ahead and climbed a sycamore-fig tree beside the road, for Jesus was going to pass that way.

When Jesus came by, He looked up at Zacchaeus and called him by name. "Zacchaeus!" He said. "Quick, come down! I must be a guest in your home today."

Zacchaeus quickly climbed down and took Jesus to his house in great excitement and joy. But the people were displeased. "He has gone to be the guest of a notorious sinner," they grumbled.

Meanwhile, Zacchaeus stood before the Lord and said, "I will give half my wealth to the poor, Lord, and if I have cheated people on their taxes, I will give them back four times as much!"

Jesus responded, "Salvation has come to this home today, for this man has shown himself to be a true son of Abraham. For the Son of Man came to seek and save those who are lost." (Lk 19:2-10 NLT)

It is easy to see how Jesus delivered these people from the incarcerating power of sin that held them in bondage. You can also see that there was an effort on each one of their parts to seek and trust what Jesus said to them. We see repentance was also an action they took that brought about their deliverance and new life. Many times, we want God to do everything for us without an effort on our part, but that is not how it works. I have met many people who came to the church for deliverance and I believe God moved in their life but because there was no repentance or act of obedience on their part they simply went right back to the same old bondages. We can see how Jesus even cast demons out of people who were completely possessed, but as I will show you, there comes responsibility on our part to obey or they will come back.

As Jesus was climbing out of the boat, a man who was possessed by demons came out to meet Him. For a long time he had been homeless and naked, living in a cemetery outside the town.

As soon as he saw Jesus, he shrieked and fell down in front of Him. Then he screamed, "Why are You interfering with me, Jesus, Son of the Most High God? Please, I beg You, don't torture me!" For Jesus had already commanded the evil spirit to come out of him. This spirit had often taken control of the man. Even when he was placed under guard and put in chains and shackles, he simply broke them and rushed out into the wilderness, completely under the demon's power.

Jesus demanded, "What is your name?"

"Legion," he replied, for he was filled with many demons. The demons kept begging Jesus not to send them into the bottomless pit.

There happened to be a large herd of pigs feeding on the hillside nearby, and the demons begged Him to let them enter into the pigs.

So Jesus gave them permission. Then the demons came out of the man and entered the pigs, and the entire herd plunged down the steep hillside into the lake and drowned.

When the herdsmen saw it, they fled to the nearby town and the surrounding countryside, spreading the news as they ran. People rushed out to see what had happened. A crowd soon gathered around Jesus, and they saw the man who had been freed from the demons. He was sitting at Jesus' feet, fully clothed and perfectly sane, and they were all afraid. Then those who had seen what happened told the others how the demon-possessed man had been healed. (Lk 8:27-36 NLT)

You must notice that the man with the demons ran to meet Jesus but it was the demons that spoke through the man. The point is that even the demon-possessed man ran to the one who had the power to deliver him. When the demons were gone and the man was delivered, he sat at the feet of Jesus. Too many people want to be delivered but don't want to sit at the feet of Jesus and learn from His words. They want to be delivered but don't want to live for Him and follow Him.

I must warn you that there is a great danger in seeking deliverance and not following Jesus afterward. Jesus warns us about this and tells us that our condition can become worse than before.

For when a strong man [like Satan] is fully armed and guards his palace, his possessions are safe—until someone even stronger attacks and overpowers him, strips him of his weapons, and carries off his belongings.

"Anyone who isn't with Me opposes Me, and anyone who isn't working with Me is actually working against Me.

"When an evil spirit leaves a person, it goes into the desert, searching for rest. But when it finds none, it says, 'I will return to the person I came from.' So it returns and finds that its former home is all swept and in order. Then the spirit finds seven other spirits more evil than itself, and they all enter the person and live there. And so that person is worse off than before." (Lk 11:21-26 NLT)

We must yield our lives in obedience to Jesus and His will for our lives on a daily basis if we want to remain delivered from the power of addiction and the works of Satan and demons in our lives.

Another example of this is King Saul, who was tormented by an evil spirit. David would come and play music, and the spirit would leave, only to return later. This is because Saul never repented and lived in obedience to the will of God. One thing I have observed over the many years of working in addiction recovery is that people will come to church and feel God and even be touched by God and leave a service thinking everything is okay. They believe they are free and delivered only to find out they are not free and were never delivered because they never surrendered to God's will.

Countless books have been written about spiritual warfare. Unfortunately, a simple teaching has been made very complicated and ineffective. These philosophies and teachings may sell books, but they will not get you delivered. Let me sum up spiritual warfare with a couple of verses and show you how to have victory over Satan.

> You adulterous people, don't you know that friendship with the world means enmity against God? Therefore, anyone who chooses to be a friend of the world becomes an enemy of God. Or do you think Scripture says without reason that He jealously longs for the spirit He has caused to dwell in us? But He gives us more grace. That is why Scripture says:
> "God opposes the proud
> but shows favor to the humble."
> Submit yourselves, then, to God. Resist the devil, and he will flee from you.
> Come near to God and He will come near to you. Wash your hands, you sinners, and purify your hearts, you double-minded. (Jas 4:4-8 NIV)

The key to winning the spiritual battle is to humble yourself and submit to God and resist the devil and he will flee. Seek the Lord at all times, and you will find that you may be at war from time to time but you will win all the time if you follow these simple steps.

# CHAPTER 11

## An Outward Manifestation of an Inward Transformation

By the time you get to this chapter, you should be fully aware of the miracle that has taken place in you and continues to happen daily as God is changing you into His own image. You are now a child of God, chosen by God, justified by God, and being glorified by God. You are a new creation, a Royal Priesthood, a Holy Generation. You are a part of God's Glorious Kingdom and flesh of His flesh and bone of His bone, a part of the Body of Christ. This kind of continual inward transformation will certainly begin to manifest outwardly in your conduct, behavior, and way of living. People are probably noticing the change that is happening in your life just by the way you live. As much as the transforming power of God changes our morality, it changes other aspects of our life as well. You should see your self-esteem, self-worth, and confidence building as your relationship with God grows. If we are the children of God and a nation of Kings and Priests, then we need to reflect that in every aspect of our life. Not in a way that exudes pride, elitism, or arrogance, but in a way that mirrors the nature of our God. It should show in how you carry yourself, how you appear, and the self-respect you hold as you allow God to fashion you as He intended. Many times, addictions rob you of confidence, self-esteem, and self-worth, and it reflects in the way you look, dress, and carry yourself. If you are representing God, then you want to look and carry yourself in a way that reflects Him and His excellence. The Bible says that we are His ambassadors, which means we are His representatives.

"So we are Christ's ambassadors; God is making His appeal through us. We speak for Christ when we plead, 'Come back to God!'" (2 Cor 5:20 NLT).

As His representatives, we need to have good personal hygiene that reflects in our personal appearance. We need to dress as His representatives so that people will take us seriously and know that we respect ourselves. This does not mean that I have to wear a designer suit, and it certainly doesn't mean we become vain and outward-focused, but it does mean we should look presentable and respectful.

I want to share my personal testimony that happened to me after I was saved and started in the ministry. I, too, came from a background of addiction and a dysfunctional lifestyle, but it has never kept me from having an effective ministry that has touched millions of lives worldwide. God has used me to minister to the most broken people in society and to professional people such as judges, politicians, and wealthy businesspeople. God wants to use you to touch people from all walks of life and people from every cultural and social background. I had been pastoring for almost three years when a close friend approached me and was brutally honest with me about my appearance. I once looked and dressed more like a biker than someone who was in the ministry; that is not to cast any negative reflection on bikers. I was just being who and what I thought I was, but his statement would change my perception and the course of my ministry. He said to me that because of the way I dressed and appeared, I would never be able to minister to him if he had not known my story simply because of the way I looked. He went on to share that I was closing a door to minister to people from all walks of life as well as causing some people to not take me seriously. He stated that I did not have to look like a biker all the time but that it was okay to dress differently and change my appearance so that I could minister to all people from all walks of life instead of people like myself. He was not saying that I should abandon my jeans and Harley shirts but just simply have diversity in my appearance to reach more people, which is what God wants. I took what he said to heart and began to make changes. The results were staggering. I was taken seriously by more people, and doors began to open for me that I never saw myself being able to walk through. I still, to this day, put on my leather and ride my Harley, but that is not my identity. My identity is in Christ, and I can become all things to all men that I may win some to Christ. God wants to open doors for you to have more relationships with an array of people as well as advance you in your career and social influence. For this to happen, you must consider how you carry yourself and how you present yourself. Some may say this counsel is asking people to be something they are not, but that is far from the truth. You are not the person you used to be, and you should not let something as simple as outward appearance close a door God wants to open for you. Let's face it—our society places emphasis on outward appearance. Employers, law enforcement, everyday people, and even the cashier at a retail store will judge you based on appearance regardless of whether it is right or wrong; it is a fact of life. If my greatest goal in life is to honor God in everything I do, taking pride in personal appearance should not be a stumbling block. In truth, I really don't want people to identify me as the person I once was, although my heart desires to minister to people who are where I once was. I found that I could come out from among everything that reflects my old life so that people no longer identify me as that old person I used to be but still go back and minister to people that were just like I once was. I am reminded of a Scripture that says just that.

"Therefore, come out from among unbelievers, and separate yourselves from them, says the LORD. Don't touch their filthy things, and I will welcome you. And I will be your Father, and you will be My sons and daughters, says the LORD Almighty" (2 Cor 6:17-18 NLT). In closing I want to encourage you to embrace the new life God has given you and welcome the new things He has prepared for you. There is no limit to what God will do for you and through you, so hold your head high and know that you are a child of God created in His image and destined to fulfill His Kingdom purpose for your life.

# CHAPTER 12

## Forgiveness and Forgiving

We touched on this subject in our chapter on prayer, but it is important to take a closer look at forgiveness and forgiving because it is a key to overcoming addiction and living a life free from it. For us to understand how to forgive others, we must first understand the forgiveness God has provided for us. Many times it is the hurts and wounds of our past that have resulted in the addictions we struggle with. It could be the abandonment of a parent, spouse, or friend. It could be the pain of molestation or sexual violation. In a fallen world, many vile actions are done that wound us emotionally, mentally, and even physically, and the results can be that we medicate ourselves with mind-altering substances to help ease the pain. Most people did not set out to become an addict but unfortunately the end result is addiction. It is easy to think about what someone else has done to us or what an unjust situation did to us, but the truth is we have all done our share of wrongs. No one is truly innocent of hurting people or causing others pain, loss, and disappointment. Truth is, our addictions have hurt those who love us most. They, too, have felt betrayed, let down, and discouraged as a result of our behavior. Even though we too have done these things, God has chosen to love you and forgive you even though we do not deserve this generosity of mercy and forgiveness. As bad as we can ever be, God never gives up on us. He showed you mercy long before you repented and turned to Him. In fact, Jesus died for us while we were yet sinners, showing us a demonstration of love knowing some would never accept it and repent.

"Now, most people would not be willing to die for an upright person, though someone might perhaps be willing to die for a person who is especially good. But God showed His great love for us by sending Christ to die for us while we were still sinners" (Rom 5:7-8 NLT).

When God forgave us, He took away the sins we committed with the price of the blood of Jesus. He put us in right standing with Himself, even though we did nothing to deserve this kind of mercy. His forgiveness took away our sins and faults and buried them in the depths of the sea and cast them as far as the east is from the west.

59

"Where is another God like You, who pardons the guilt of the remnant, overlooking the sins of His special people? You will not stay angry with Your people forever, because You delight in showing unfailing love. Once again You will have compassion on us. You will trample our sins under Your feet and throw them into the depths of the ocean! You will show us Your faithfulness and unfailing love as You promised to our ancestors Abraham and Jacob long ago" (Mi 7:18-20 NLT).

Psalm 103:8-14 (NLT) tells us, "The LORD is compassionate and merciful, slow to get angry and filled with unfailing love. He will not constantly accuse us, nor remain angry forever. He does not punish us for all our sins; He does not deal harshly with us, as we deserve. For His unfailing love toward those who fear Him is as great as the height of the heavens above the earth. He has removed our sins as far from us as the east is from the west. The LORD is like a father to His children, tender and compassionate to those who fear Him. For He knows how weak we are; He remembers we are only dust."

He never gave up on us even when we were at our most rebellious state, caring only for ourselves. He gave us patience and time we did not deserve.

"The Lord isn't really being slow about His promise, as some people think. No, He is being patient for your sake. He does not want anyone to be destroyed, but wants everyone to repent" (2 Pt 3:9 NLT).

We see this illustrated in the parable of the lost sheep when He said He would leave the ninety-nine and go into the wilderness and search for it UNTIL He found the one. He patiently searched for us, not giving up but extending mercy.

"If a man has a hundred sheep and one of them gets lost, what will he do? Won't he leave the ninety-nine others in the wilderness and go to search for the one that is lost until he finds it? And when he has found it, he will joyfully carry it home on his shoulders. When he arrives, he will call together his friends and neighbors, saying, 'Rejoice with me because I have found my lost sheep'" (Lk 15:4-6 NLT).

As we have received patience, mercy, and forgiveness, we should also extend that same kind of patience, mercy, and forgiveness to ourselves and others. Jesus taught us that we must extend forgiveness in the same way He did to us. There are people in our lives who have not asked us to forgive them and some that may never be able to repent or ask for our forgiveness, but we must extend mercy to them so we can move on with our lives. The Scriptures teach us that we are to pray for people who have misused us and even pray for our enemies.

> "But to you who are willing to listen, I say, love your enemies! Do good to those who hate you. Bless those who curse you. Pray for those who hurt you. If someone slaps you on one cheek, offer the other cheek also. If someone demands your coat, offer your shirt also. Give to anyone who asks; and when things are taken away from you, don't try to get them back. Do to others as you would like them to do to you.
>
> "If you love only those who love you, why should you get credit for that? Even sinners love those who love them! And if you do good only to those who do good to you, why should you get credit? Even sinners do that much! And if you lend money only to those who can repay you, why should you get credit? Even sinners will lend to other sinners for a full return.
>
> "Love your enemies! Do good to them. Lend to them without expecting to be repaid. Then your reward from heaven will be very great, and you will truly be acting as children of the Most High, for He is kind to those who are unthankful and wicked. You must be compassionate, just as your Father is compassionate." (Lk 6:27-36 NLT)

You may ask, "Why should we show this kindness to people who would not show it to us?" You should because Christ has shown it to you undeservingly. You must understand that holding onto unforgiveness and past wrongs only hurts you. You are giving the person who hurt you or wronged you control over your life. They continue to hold your thoughts and actions hostage while they move on with their life; I do not think anyone would want to give this kind of control to anyone but Jesus. When the hurts of yesterday control your decisions, behavior, emotions, and thoughts, then you are actually a slave to that person and their actions. Jesus taught us that this would happen if we don't extend mercy and forgiveness. We can see that forgiveness is not just about the person we are forgiving but it is about our own well-being and freedom.

61

"Therefore, the Kingdom of Heaven can be compared to a king who decided to bring his accounts up to date with servants who had borrowed money from him. In the process, one of his debtors was brought in who owed him millions of dollars. He couldn't pay, so his master ordered that he be sold—along with his wife, his children, and everything he owned—to pay the debt.

"But the man fell down before his master and begged him, 'Please, be patient with me, and I will pay it all.' Then his master was filled with pity for him, and he released him and forgave his debt.

"But when the man left the king, he went to a fellow servant who owed him a few thousand dollars. He grabbed him by the throat and demanded instant payment.

"His fellow servant fell down before him and begged for a little more time. 'Be patient with me, and I will pay it,' he pleaded. But his creditor wouldn't wait. He had the man arrested and put in prison until the debt could be paid in full.

"When some of the other servants saw this, they were very upset. They went to the king and told him everything that had happened. Then the king called in the man he had forgiven and said, 'You evil servant! I forgave you that tremendous debt because you pleaded with me. Shouldn't you have mercy on your fellow servant, just as I had mercy on you?' Then the angry king sent the man to prison to be tortured until he had paid his entire debt.

"That's what My heavenly Father will do to you if you refuse to forgive your brothers and sisters from your heart." (Mt 18:23-35 NLT)

You may think that you cannot forgive a person, and the fact is you cannot by your own ability. But with the grace and power of God, you can. To receive this grace and power, we must do what Jesus says we should do. We must begin to pray for those individuals and show compassion; God's grace and power will eventually take over and you will find yourself overcoming the pain and showing the right heart toward those who hurt you and you will ultimately be set free from the bondage that held your mind, thoughts, and emotions captive.

If we intend to be free from addiction and remain free, we must then use this key of knowledge and forgive those whose actions have resulted in our wrong behavior.

# CHAPTER 13

## Forgetting the Past and Embracing the Future

Your past does not define you. Because of what Christ has done for you and continues to do, your past will not determine your future. Forgetting your past is yet another key to living a life free from addiction. One of the amazing things Christ has provided for us is to become a brand-new person; however, for that to be manifest in us the old things must pass away.

"This means that anyone who belongs to Christ has become a new person. The old life is gone; a new life has begun!" (2 Cor 5:17 NLT).

If we are not willing to let go of our past life, identity, personality, behavior, mind-sets, and perceptions, then the new person God has created us to be will not survive long and relapse will be inevitable. Understanding that we are not that old person we used to be is a huge step toward being able to embrace the new man/woman God has destined us to become.

The Apostle Paul was one of the most notorious sinners we find in the Bible, and he did all his wrong in the name of religion. He was a persecutor of the church and was even responsible for the death of Stephen, one of the disciples. He had climbed high up the ladder of Judaism as one of the most educated Pharisees among the Jews, with tremendous respect from the Jews and their leaders. He was accepted by many religious people and had quite the reputation to uphold and protect. You could say he was very rooted in his identity as a Jew and knew no other life. Yet, when he encountered Jesus on the road to Damascus, everything changed; Paul describes who he once was and how he feels about that person compared to the new person God has made him to be. He also tells us how important it is for us to forget that old person and lifestyle. Let's look at Paul's testimony.

For we who worship by the Spirit of God are the ones who are truly circumcised. We rely on what Christ Jesus has done for us. We put no confidence in human effort, though I could have confidence in my own effort if anyone could. Indeed, if others have reason for confidence in their own efforts, I have even more!

I was circumcised when I was eight days old. I am a pure-blooded citizen of Israel and a member of the tribe of Benjamin—a real Hebrew if there ever was one! I was a member of the Pharisees, who demand the strictest obedience to the Jewish law. I was so zealous that I harshly persecuted the church. And as for righteousness, I obeyed the law without fault.

I once thought these things were valuable, but now I consider them worthless because of what Christ has done. Yes, everything else is worthless when compared with the infinite value of knowing Christ Jesus my Lord. For His sake I have discarded everything else, counting it all as garbage, so that I could gain Christ. (Phil 3:3-8 NLT)

I want to point out several things from Paul's testimony that will help us to put our past behind us.

1. He had made a tremendous reputation for himself through his own abilities and efforts. You also have created your reputation, and some of it came from your family lineage and way of life just as Paul's did. You may not be happy about some of the things you have done but that old person you once were still has a place of familiarity and a social environment that supports and upholds that old life.
2. Paul once thought that these things he was and had accomplished were valuable; you, too, may still hold some value to your past. Paul says that he now counts all this as worthless. What caused him to have this change of thinking?
3. These things he once was and had achieved became worthless when he compared them to the infinite value of knowing Christ Jesus, his Lord. Understanding who and what God has destined for you is of such a greater value than anything you ever were or had ever achieved. To be able to see and understand who He has created you to be is the key to devaluing your old life and leaving it behind.
4. Paul says for Jesus's sake he discarded his old life and counted it as garbage. You will find that Jesus taught us that if we would give up our old life He would give us His life. When we understand Him and

all that He is, we then understand who we are destined to become like because we are created in His image.

"If you cling to your life, you will lose it; but if you give up your life for Me, you will find it" (Mt 10:39 NLT).

When we give up our old life we find the true life that God has predestined us to have (Rom 8:29).

In Christ, the Apostle Paul accomplished great things and was used in a way that may seem unimaginable to most. Yet, he made this profound statement: "The ONE thing I do: forgetting those things that are behind me and reaching to those things which are before me." When a man as accomplished as the Apostle Paul tells us the ONE thing he does, we must pay attention.

"Not as though I had already attained, either were already perfect: but I follow after, if that I may apprehend that for which also I am apprehended of Christ Jesus. Brethren, I count not myself to have apprehended: but this one thing I do, forgetting those things which are behind, and reaching forth unto those things which are before" (Phil 3:12-13 KJV).

Paul says he had not understood all that God had apprehended him for but he knew the ability to do so would depend on him forgetting the things that were behind him. He goes on to reveal what motivated him to forget his old life and that was the prize of the high calling of God.

"I press toward the mark for the prize of the high calling of God in Christ Jesus" (Phil 3:14 KJV).

Paul said he had to press toward the mark of the high calling, meaning he had to stretch and exert himself to reach this mark. We, too, must keep the prize before us and put all of our efforts and energy in obtaining who God has destined us to become and accomplishing His purpose for our life.

As you continue moving forward toward that new person and new purpose, you will find that the old man and old way of life is no longer familiar to you and that you have nothing in common with it. It will lose all value to you.

# CHAPTER 14

## Recognizing and Overcoming Insecurity

Insecurity is subtle and sometimes an overlooked problem that feeds and fuels addiction, so one of the keys to conquering addiction is to recognize and overcome insecurity. Insecurity can come as a result of many things, such as abandonment, lack of parental support, mental and physical abuse, molestation, or any other tragic event that may have occurred in our lives. It can be the cause of self-medicating with illegal drugs, prescription drugs, alcohol, or even sexual acts, and this leads to addiction.

The first thing a person must do is recognize the insecurity; this is done by recognizing the behavior it creates. We will take a look at some of these behaviors so you can identify it in your life.

Insecurity is like any other thing the enemy uses against God's people, and its strength is in its ability to go unrecognized. Denial or not recognizing a problem can make it impossible to be healed.

Signs of Insecurity

☐ An insecure person becomes overtly selfish. He/She tries to surround himself/herself with possessions, accolades, and attention. Abundance makes him/her secure and feel protected. When he/she has got many friends and a lot of money to support his/her life, he/she feels like nothing can get him/her. It is obviously a wrong sense of security because it depends on external factors.

☐ An insecure person becomes overly accommodating and tries to gain other people's approval. Validation is what insecure people covet all the time. They go out of their way to get appreciation. They want to be accepted by everyone to feel secure. If someone is indifferent or does not give approval, insecure people get stuck on the idea of getting consent from this particular person.

☐ Insecure people tend to be very defensive and cannot handle criticism. They are not comfortable with their own self. When someone constructively criticizes them, they take it as a personal attack. Insecure people have a tendency to take everything personally. Even if the criticism is not directly on them but on things involving them, they take it on themselves. It is very difficult to hold a constructive conversation with an insecure person.

☐ An insecure person who is in denial about the insecurity will often vocalize that he/she does not want attention, accolades, approval, or even appreciation, but he/she will become very offended if he/she does not receive it.

☐ An insecure person will go to great extremes to be the center of attention by whatever means necessary at every opportunity and occasion.

☐ An insecure person will go to the extreme to win your approval but will then gossip behind your back if it will help him/her to be validated by someone else. He/She is only loyal if it means having a person's approval or validation.

☐ An insecure person will not usually have lifelong relationships. This can also include family. He/She may even have a long list of broken marriages.

☐ Insecure people can't enjoy silence and they try to fill it with unnecessary chatter. This is because they find it very hard to stay with their thoughts. They do not have a very positive view on themselves; therefore whenever they just sit in silence, their minds tend to go back to the thoughts they have been ignoring about themselves. This makes insecure people uncomfortable, which is why they are always talking or spending time with everyone else but themselves.

☐ Excessive joking is also a mechanism for coping with insecurity. An insecure person craves other people's attention, which is achieved when other people laugh at their jokes. However, this leads to insensitivity toward others. Not just making fun of others, insecure people also make fun of themselves constantly to grab some attention. They have an attention-seeking attitude; they use anything and everything for it. In fact, sometimes they resort to cruel attitudes as well. For example, if their peers are bullying someone, their sense of wrong and right will be clouded due to insecurity and desperation to fit in and they will go along with it instead of standing against it.

☐ Insecure people are self-promoting and constantly talk about themselves. They need validation from other people for their actions and qualities. They do not listen to or pay attention to other people's stories and opinions but only think of their own problems and situations.

- Insecure people are threatened by others and they try to crush their opinions by bullying. They are either very competitive or suck up very easily to the people who are in authority.
- Insecure people tend to be overly authoritative; they tend to compensate for their lack of confidence by taking out their frustrations on their subordinates. They feel more powerful in other people's docility for them.

- They cannot stand a defeat. They are scared of losing so they always keep themselves at the edge.
- Extreme jealousy is yet another sign of insecure people as they lack trust in their partners. This is visible in constant questioning, mistrust, and altercations with members of the opposite sex. They are jealous of coworkers and are threatened by other talented people.
- When an insecure person is in a place of authority, they may attempt to hold back or oppress talented and highly potential people regardless of the contribution they could make.
- Insecure people may even become abusive if they fail to control their partners or close friends.
- Insecure people can sometimes attempt to be overachievers and take on too many responsibilities in an attempt to be validated, feel accepted or important in the eyes of others.
- Many times, they will complain to others about their excessive workload that they brought on themselves in an attempt to get sympathy or attention from people.
- Overly sexual behavior also portrays insecurity as the person treats his or her sexuality as a crutch to get others' attention. For them, sex is just another way to win and prove their courage.

What do chronically insecure people believe?

- I can never accomplish the task facing me. (Although they will take on many as an effort to feel accepted or accomplished.)

71

- [ ] Everybody is looking at me; they are just waiting for me to make a fool of myself.

- [ ] I am a failure.

- [ ] I am ugly and awful to look at.

- [ ] I can never win. I am a loser.

- [ ] What is the sense of trying when I'll never get it right?

- [ ] No matter how hard I work to achieve, I never get any recognition.

- [ ] I am incompetent in everything.

- [ ] How could anybody ever say anything good about me?

- [ ] I failed them in the past; therefore, I am a failure today.

- [ ] Once a failure, always a failure.

- [ ] There is only one direction for me to go in this organization, and that is down and out.

- [ ] No one could ever like, respect, or accept me.

- [ ] I don't deserve to be treated nicely.

- [ ] I don't fit in here, or anywhere else, for that matter.

- [ ] Everyone else looks so good, so together; I feel so out of it compared to them.

- [ ] I am an incomplete person and will always be that way.

- [ ] I am so afraid that no one will like me.

- [ ] Why would anyone care to hear what I say, how I feel, or what I think?

- [ ] People are just nice to you in order to use you and get something they want from you.

One of the clearest examples of insecurity found in the Bible is seen in King Saul. We see insecurity at work in his life when the well-known prophet and man of God called him to be king and he began to make excuses as to why he was not the man for the calling. He actually ran and hid himself among the baggage. We also see it later when the Prophet Samuel confronted Saul about his disobedience.

In 1 Samuel 9:19-21 (NLT):

"I am the seer!" Samuel replied. "Go up to the place of worship ahead of me. We will eat there together, and in the morning I'll tell you what you want to know and send you on your way. And don't worry about those donkeys that were lost three days ago, for they have been found. And I am here to tell you that you and your family are the focus of all Israel's hopes."

Saul replied, "But I'm only from the tribe of Benjamin, the smallest tribe in Israel, and my family is the least important of all the families of that tribe! Why are you talking like this to me?"

Later, in 1 Samuel 10:21-23 (NLT), we learn how "he brought each family of the tribe of Benjamin before the LORD, and the family of the Matrites was chosen. And finally Saul son of Kish was chosen from among them. But when they looked for him, he had disappeared! So they asked the LORD, "Where is he?" And the LORD replied, "He is hiding among the baggage." So they found him and brought him out, and he stood head and shoulders above anyone else.

In 1 Samuel 15:17 (NLT), "Samuel told him, 'Although you may think little of yourself, are you not the leader of the tribes of Israel? The LORD has anointed you king of Israel.'"

The signs and effects of Saul's insecurity.

1. Saul initially clung to David because of the benefit David brought him.
2. Saul would later become jealous of David because of his success. "So from that time on Saul kept a jealous eye on David" (1 Sm 18:9 NLT).

3. Saul actually tried to secretly kill David, despite the fact that he was a great friend and benefit for him and for Israel.
4. Saul took credit for his son's victory over the Philistine garrison. (1 Sm 13:1-4 NLT)
5. He tried to perform a sacrifice that was meant for a priest only. (He would not make room for another person's gifting.)
6. Saul made a foolish oath by making his army fast when they were already exhausted. Yet, instead of admitting he was wrong, he would have allowed his son to die. (1 Sm 14)
7. Saul disobeyed the commandment of God to please the people. "Then Saul admitted to Samuel, 'Yes, I have sinned. I have disobeyed your instructions and the LORD's command, for I was afraid of the people and did what they demanded. But now, please forgive my sin and come back with me so that I may worship the LORD'" (1 Sm 15:24-25 NLT).
8. He was more concerned about how people viewed him than the fact that God had rejected him. "Then Saul pleaded again, 'I know I have sinned. But please, at least honor me before the elders of my people and before Israel by coming back with me so that I may worship the LORD your God'" (1 Sm 15:30 NLT).

Saul's insecurity led to a demonic stronghold.

1. The Bible teaches us that we should not make a place or a door for Satan to enter our life, but Saul did just that. "Now the Spirit of the LORD had left Saul, and the LORD sent a tormenting spirit that filled him with depression and fear" (1 Sm 16:14 NLT).
2. Saul was later involved in witchcraft when he consulted a medium to call back Samuel from the dead (1 Sm 28:7-11).

Further Causes and Effects of Insecurity:

The king then asked him, "Is anyone still alive from Saul's family? If so, I want to show God's kindness to them."
Ziba replied, "Yes, one of Jonathan's sons is still alive. He is crippled in both feet."
"Where is he?" the king asked.
"In Lo-debar," Ziba told him, "at the home of Makir son

of Ammiel."

So David sent for him and brought him from Makir's home. His name was Mephibosheth; he was Jonathan's son and Saul's grandson. When he came to David, he bowed low to the ground in deep respect. David said, "Greetings, Mephibosheth."

Mephibosheth replied, "I am your servant."

"Don't be afraid!" David said. "I intend to show kindness to you because of my promise to your father, Jonathan. I will give you all the property that once belonged to your grandfather Saul, and you will eat here with me at the king's table!"

Mephibosheth bowed respectfully and exclaimed, "Who is your servant, that you should show such kindness to a dead dog like me?" (2 Sm 9:3-8 NLT)

We learn how his affliction came to be, and it, too, is tied to the theme of insecurity. "Saul's son Jonathan had a son named Mephibosheth, who was crippled as a child. He was five years old when the report came from Jezreel that Saul and Jonathan had been killed in battle. (When the child's nurse heard the news, she picked him up and fled. But as she hurried away, she dropped him, and he became crippled)" (2 Sm 4:4 NLT).

Insecurity is a subtle danger. In order to recognize this problem in our lives, we must take an honest look at where it originates. Let's identify some common causes for a lack of confidence.

1. Insecurity grows out of a persistent sense of being unaccepted. When we grow up thinking no one really likes us, we turn into chronically shy, unconfident adults. This can come from a parent or parents who continually put us down, being picked on as a child, or being a child who is physically abused or molested.

2. Tragedy can initiate such feelings. Broken homes, the death of a loved one, and other relationship scars can be causes.

3. A poor body image can damage self-esteem. The issue may be body shape, weight, birthmarks, hair loss, or anything else that leads people to see themselves in a negative light. The result is a sense of shame and self-consciousness that permeates every personal interaction.

4.  Insecure individuals often have a history of feeling overshadowed by others. When this happens, they are preoccupied with people who seem smarter, wealthier, nicer-looking, more successful, and so on. This creates doubt in their ability to achieve anything themselves.

5.  A serious "life failure" can result in a tremendous loss of self-esteem. When we pour ourselves into our work and families, a setback in these areas has the potential of crushing our spirits.

More Effects of Insecurity:

☐   Difficulties in establishing healthy, long-lasting relationships.

☐   Being perceived incorrectly by others as being snobbish or uppity.

☐   Becoming victims of fears that impair their freedom of action or choice.

☐   Being candidates for paranoia and feeling others are out to get them.

☐   Scaring others away from them by their defensive attitude.

☐   Being overly controlled emotionally, having problems letting others in on their emotions.
This can lead others to guess what is going on until the passivity of the insecure person leads to an overreaction by the others, resulting in conflict or rejection.

☐   Having problems on the job or in school when they have the knowledge, skills, and abilities to do a task efficiently but are told to do it in a different, less effective manner. They get so uptight about the job and are fearful of standing up for what they believe that they get angry, hostile, and resentful until they either quit or succeed in submerging their emotions.

☐   Getting passed over for promotions, advances, or honors because they are so quiet about what it is they do. This leads the insecure persons to feel more unaccepted, unappreciated, and undervalued.

☐   Having problems meeting people and often can become debilitated socially by chronic shyness.

☐   Becoming so inward that they seek to escape into their fantasy life rather than deal with the reality of their lives.

How Insecurity Affects Marriage and Intimate Relationships:

- ☐ "I am not good enough." It is true that you must learn to love yourself before you can truly be satisfied in an intimate relationship. Most people are attracted to partners who are confident, joyful, and independent. If you are constantly down on yourself, how can you expect your partner to not start feeling the same way? Accentuate the positive, not only for the benefit of your own self-esteem, but also so your partner can focus on the things he/she loves about you.
- ☐ "I bet she/he is cheating on me." Take a moment to think about why you feel this way. Has your partner given you a reason to believe that there is infidelity taking place? Or is it your insecurity speaking? Jealousy and resentment are relationship killers. Trust is a huge aspect of a healthy relationship. Once you tackle your insecurities, your ability to trust will also improve and your relationship will benefit.
- ☐ "I need to know what he/she is thinking." Constantly worrying about what your partner is thinking is only going to weigh you down with anxiety. When your partner says one thing, don't assume he/she means something different or is trying to hide something from you. Repeatedly asking your partner what he/she is thinking or feeling is an energy drainer on you both and will likely cause your partner to be even more withdrawn. Everyone deserves the right to privacy and unspoken thoughts.
- ☐ "I need constant communication/interaction." Just like anything that grows, a relationship needs proper space to flourish. Don't fret if you don't get that call or text when you think you should or if your partner needs to reschedule plans. Participate in your own activities and hobbies and let your partner do the same. You and your partner will both benefit from having space from one another, and it will make your relationship stronger.
- ☐ "This relationship is just like my last one." Avoid comparing your current relationship to past ones. Saying things like, "You are acting just like my ex-girlfriend," or "You're going to end up leaving me like he/she did," can be very hurtful. Even if a past partner was

abusive, unfaithful, critical, or dishonest, it doesn't mean that your current partner is that way. It may be difficult at times, but try your best to focus on your current relationship and leave your baggage at the door.

How Insecurity Affects Friendships, Social, and Professional Relationships:

☐ The need to control: Insecure people can often have an overwhelming desire to control the relationships around them and situations that are being presented to them. Insecurities can make a person feel as if he/she is constantly walking outside of his comfort zone, and we all know how that feels. Because of this, insecure people will often desperately try to control the views, opinions, and actions of others. They always need to be right and never wrong. Insecure people will often need to have the last word and will sometimes find it hard to accept others' views or opinions, often believing their view is the only correct viewpoint. They will also often get very frustrated if others express a different opinion or even challenge their own beliefs.

☐ Finger pointing and fault-finding: Insecure people will often blame others for their own unhappiness and insecurities. Secure, happy, and confident people may not always be happy with a certain situation, but they won't always be looking to point the blame at everyone else. This is something I have dealt with on many, many occasions as a manager. The classic excuse of "It's so-and-so's fault I'm unhappy because she didn't do this or that" is common in insecure people.

☐ Not wanting to share happiness or success: This is a common cause for friendships and partnerships to break down; one person's insecurities inhibits his/her ability to be happy for someone else's good fortune or success. You may have been friends with someone for a while, or in a relationship that was ticking along nicely, and then suddenly your situation changes, and your partner or friend begins to find it difficult to share your happiness. You may get a new job, find a new boyfriend/girlfriend, buy your dream home, and

78

before you know it your friend, for no obvious reason, no longer wants to spend time with you. This can be hurtful and confusing. Your partner/friend may be struggling with feelings of worthlessness, unhappiness, and jealousy and finds it difficult to see you spending time with your new man/woman, enjoying your new job, and so on. For you, it can leave you feeling hurt and confused that your friend, who you valued, suddenly can't be happy for you. Insecure people can feel threatened very easily, and will often struggle to keep the upper hand when it comes to their careers, relationships, and personal life as this gives them a sense of worth. Insecure people can also often shut down and appear to turn on you for no real valid reason because they are finding it increasingly challenging and difficult to deal with their negative feelings and emotions.

☐ Bouts of anger or frustration: Ultimately, insecurities are formed from our childhood experiences and situations that we have faced in our younger years. Insecure people are still holding onto experiences, which affect how they interact in the world as adults. Because of their insecurities, they may find it difficult to extend love and instead they choose to extend anger and frustration.

☐ Encrypted social media rants: I suppose I am not surprised at the amount of people who turn to their social media sites to post encrypted rants about things they are unhappy with, but I really don't see how it benefits anyone. Other than getting a few things off of your chest in a public forum for the world to see, how does that serve anyone well? I personally feel, if you have a friend or partner who feels the need to do this, do not get into a conversation with him/her about it online, or comment on his/her post. Encouraging such negativity in fact just feeds the negativity, and in turn empowers it even more. Secure, confident people, who value your friendship, will have the decency to talk to you face to face about something you may or may not have done that has caused them upset. Random ranting posts are just screaming for attention.

Now that we have identified how insecurity manifests and what it can lead to, we must be healed from it in order for it to no longer affect our lives and cause destructive behavior. One major key to being healed of insecurity is forgiveness, which we have already covered, but I want to discuss it further as it relates to insecurity.

An individual must be willing to forgive oneself as Christ has forgiven him/her. Jesus paid the ultimate price for our forgiveness, and to not forgive ourselves would be an injustice to God because He loved us enough to provide the blood of His son to give us the gift of forgiveness. What Jesus did for us through His death and resurrection was to remove all the condemnation and judgment against us.

"You were dead because of your sins and because your sinful nature was not yet cut away. Then God made you alive with Christ, for He forgave all our sins. He canceled the record of the charges against us and took it away by nailing it to the cross" (Col 2:13-14 NLT).

If God no longer condemns us, we should not condemn ourselves because we have been forgiven and made to be a new creation.

"There is therefore now no condemnation to them which are in Christ Jesus, who walk not after the flesh, but after the Spirit" (Rom 8:1 KJV).

We must forgive those who have hurt us and wronged us, just as God has forgiven us. (See chapter on Forgiveness and Forgiving.)

God has provided healing and deliverance through Jesus Christ. We must receive that gift so that we can move forward in a victorious life no longer bound to insecurity and addiction.

"He personally carried our sins in His body on the cross so that we can be dead to sin and live for what is right. By His wounds you are healed" (1 Pt 2:24 NLT).

"Are any of you sick? You should call for the elders of the church to come and pray over you, anointing you with oil in the name of the Lord. Such a prayer offered in faith will heal the sick, and the Lord will make you well. And if you have committed any sins, you will be forgiven" (Jas 5:14-15 NLT).

# CHAPTER 15

## Stay Filled with the Holy Spirit

It is obvious through past chapters that the Holy Spirit is one of the most significant keys to walking in the strength and power of God so that we are no longer slaves to any addiction and to living a victorious and overcoming life. First, we must understand that the Holy Spirit is God and His form of being in constant communion and fellowship with us. It is through the work of the Holy Spirit that we are born-again, creating the change in our lives and restoring the image of God in us. Second, we must understand that it is the Holy Spirit that empowers and enables us to live a life pleasing to God. Third, we must understand that the Holy Spirit is what equips and empowers us with gifts to fulfill His purpose and do the work He has created us to do. Below are Scriptures that validate the importance and purpose of the Holy Spirit.

Jesus replied, "I tell you the truth, unless you are born again, you cannot see the Kingdom of God."

"What do You mean?" exclaimed Nicodemus. "How can an old man go back into his mother's womb and be born again?"

Jesus replied, "I assure you, no one can enter the Kingdom of God without being born of water and the Spirit. Humans can reproduce only human life, but the Holy Spirit gives birth to spiritual life. So don't be surprised when I say, 'You must be born again.' The wind blows wherever it wants. Just as you can hear the wind but can't tell where it comes from or where it is going, so you can't explain how people are born of the Spirit." (Jn 3:3-8 NLT)

But in fact, it is best for you that I go away, because if I don't, the Advocate won't come. If I do go away, then I will send Him to you. And when He comes, He will convict the world of its sin, and of God's righteousness, and of the coming judgment. The world's sin is that it refuses to believe in Me. Righteousness is available because I go to the Father, and you will see Me no more. Judgment will come because the ruler of this world has already been judged.

"There is so much more I want to tell you, but you can't bear it now. When the Spirit of truth comes, He will guide you into all truth. He will not speak on His own but will tell you what He has heard. He will tell you about the future. He will bring Me glory by telling you whatever He receives from Me. All that belongs to the Father is Mine; this is why I said, 'The Spirit will tell you whatever He receives from Me.' (Jn 16:7-15 NLT)

And, behold, I send the promise of My Father upon you: but tarry ye in the city of Jerusalem, until ye be endued with power from on high. (Lk 24:49 KJV)

But you will receive power when the Holy Spirit comes upon you. And you will be My witnesses, telling people about Me everywhere—in Jerusalem, throughout Judea, in Samaria, and to the ends of the earth. (Acts 1:8 NLT)

Now, dear brothers and sisters, regarding your question about the special abilities the Spirit gives us. I don't want you to misunderstand this. You know that when you were still pagans, you were led astray and swept along in worshiping speechless idols. So I want you to know that no one speaking by the Spirit of God will curse Jesus, and no one can say Jesus is Lord, except by the Holy Spirit.

There are different kinds of spiritual gifts, but the same Spirit is the source of them all. There are different kinds of service, but we serve the same Lord. God works in different ways, but it is the same God who does the work in all of us.

A spiritual gift is given to each of us so we can help each other. (1 Cor 12:1-7 NLT)

We will now look deeper into the way in which the Holy Spirit operates in our life, from spiritual conception to our daily walk with Him.

The initial way in which the Holy Spirit begins to work in us is to lead us to Jesus. Without Him, we would have never come to Jesus. It was the Spirit of God that convicted you and drew you to Jesus as your savior and Lord.

"For no one can come to Me unless the Father who sent Me draws them to Me, and at the last day I will raise them up. As it is written in the Scriptures, 'They will all be taught by God.' Everyone who listens to the Father and learns from Him comes to Me" (Jn 6:44-45 NLT).

The next work of the Holy Spirit is to bring regeneration to you, meaning the power to be born-again. According to Scripture, you exist as a body, a soul, and a spirit just as God exists as God the Father, God the Son, and God the Holy Spirit. Remember, you are created in His image, but it was the sin of Adam that contaminated us and therefore we must be born again. It is our Spirit that becomes regenerated or born-again and through this we can now be in communion and relationship with God and His will. This spiritual miracle enables us to be able to see and understand the Kingdom of God which is His will and rulership in us and in the world.

"Jesus replied, 'I tell you the truth, unless you are born again, you cannot see the Kingdom of God'" (Jn 3:3 NLT).

"Those who are dominated by the sinful nature think about sinful things, but those who are controlled by the Holy Spirit think about things that please the Spirit. So letting your sinful nature control your mind leads to death. But letting the Spirit control your mind leads to life and peace. For the sinful nature is always hostile to God. It never did obey God's laws, and it never will. That's why those who are still under the control of their sinful nature can never please God. But you are not controlled by your sinful nature. You are controlled by the Spirit if you have the Spirit of God living in you" (Rom 8:5-9 NLT). (And remember that those who do not have the Spirit of Christ living in them do not belong to Him at all.)

That is what the Scriptures mean when they say,
"No eye has seen, no ear has heard,
and no mind has imagined
what God has prepared
for those who love Him."
But it was to us that God revealed these things by His Spirit. For His Spirit searches out everything and shows us God's deep secrets. No one can know a person's thoughts except that

person's own spirit, and no one can know God's thoughts except God's own Spirit. And we have received God's Spirit (not the world's spirit), so we can know the wonderful things God has freely given us.

When we tell you these things, we do not use words that come from human wisdom. Instead, we speak words given to us by the Spirit, using the Spirit's words to explain spiritual truths. But people who aren't spiritual can't receive these truths from God's Spirit. It all sounds foolish to them and they can't understand it, for only those who are spiritual can understand what the Spirit means. Those who are spiritual can evaluate all things, but they themselves cannot be evaluated by others. For,
"Who can know the LORD's thoughts?
Who knows enough to teach Him?"
But we understand these things, for we have the mind of Christ. (1 Cor 2:9-16 NLT)

Now that we understand being born-again and how this spiritual regeneration give us understanding of God and His will, we need to see why it is important to be continually filled with the Holy Spirit as a second and continual work of the Holy Spirit that we need often. Paul writes and shows us how important it is to be continually filled with the Holy Spirit.

"Make the most of every opportunity in these evil days. Don't act thoughtlessly, but understand what the Lord wants you to do. Don't be drunk with wine because that will ruin your life. Instead, be filled with the Holy Spirit" (Eph 5:16-18 NLT).

Paul uses the analogy of being drunk with being filled with the Spirit to further show the work of the Holy Spirit and the importance being continually filled with the Spirit. When a person is drunk, he comes under the influence of the wine and it causes him to feel, act, behave, and think differently, and it changes his reasoning. Unfortunately, the change drunkenness brings isn't positive or for the good but for the worse, bringing harm, pain, regret, and despair. When we are filled with the Spirit, we come under the influence of the Spirit and it changes our behavior, thinking, and reasoning for the better and for the glory of God. We see Peter in a time of heavy persecution in Acts chapter 4 being filled with the Spirit so that he would be empowered with boldness and strength to continue the work, but I also believe to give him clear insight and strength to do what was right during such a difficult time. I also want to note that this was the third time in the book of Acts Peter was filled with the Spirit. He was first filled in Acts chapter 2, then in Acts 4:8, and we see it a fourth time in Acts 13:52.

"And when they had prayed, the place was shaken where they were assembled together; and they were all filled with the Holy Ghost, and they spake the word of God with boldness" (Acts 4:31 KJV).

Many gifts are given to us from the Holy Spirit, and these gifts are for the purpose of accomplishing God's will and purpose for our lives. Gifts are supernatural abilities given to us through the Holy Spirit for the purposes of edifying and building up the church, evangelizing and making disciples. God's Kingdom is spiritual, and it must be built by the power of the Spirit if we expect it to prevail and be as effective as God intends for it to be. You fulfilling God's purpose by being obedient to His will is critical to remaining free from addiction. When we fulfill God's will for our lives, it becomes the fulfillment we have searched for in all the wrong things that always ended up leaving us empty. Jesus told His disciples that His nourishment came from doing the will of His Father and finishing the work He was sent to do.

"Meanwhile, the disciples were urging Jesus, 'Rabbi, eat something.' But Jesus replied, 'I have a kind of food you know nothing about.' 'Did someone bring Him food while we were gone?' the disciples asked each other. Then Jesus explained: 'My nourishment comes from doing the will of God, who sent Me, and from finishing His work'" (Jn 4:31-34 NLT).

Being filled with the Spirit is as simple as asking and having faith to receive it. God desires for us to seek His infilling and longs to fill us because it is essential for us to live the life He has chosen for us.

And so I tell you, keep on asking, and you will receive what you ask for. Keep on seeking, and you will find. Keep on knocking, and the door will be opened to you. For everyone who asks, receives. Everyone who seeks, finds. And to everyone who knocks, the door will be opened.

"You fathers—if your children ask [for bread, do you give them a stone? Or if they ask] for a fish, do you give them a snake instead?

Or if they ask for an egg, do you give them a scorpion? Of course not! So if you sinful people know how to give good gifts to your children, how much more will your heavenly Father give the Holy Spirit to those who ask Him." (Lk 11:9-13 NLT)

# CHAPTER 16

## Family Relationships and Healing

Family is a vital part of our lives and can be a support system God can use to help us live a victorious life free from addiction, so it is an important key in successful recovery. They say nobody loves us like family, and I believe there is truth to that statement, but family can also hurt you more severely than anyone else. Family can be a great blessing when everyone is working together as they should, but when family relationships go off the rails, it can be a huge stumbling stone and setback.

The reason family problems can hurt us and wound us so severely is because of our expectations of family members. There is a great measure of trust and dependency placed on family relationships and rightly so because family has certain responsibilities and obligations to each other. We often forget that even though they are family, they are still human and have flaws and feelings.

All families have their share of challenges, but when addiction is involved, problems increase and so does the severity of those problems. All that we have just read about families is the reason we must strive to create a strong, healthy, and Christ-centered family.

This journey to a strong, healthy, and Christ-centered family is not always easy and unfortunately is not guaranteed, but it is certainly worth our most sincere and determined effort. In many cases, you will find that it takes much prayer, patience, mercy, and forgiveness to accomplish healing, restoration, and a healthy family unit. In most cases this is a large undertaking, so I have a little something someone once shared with me about taking on a large task such as this. He asked me, "How do you eat an elephant? One bite at a time of course." With that in mind, you must understand this will take time and you should give it your best, be patient, and celebrate the victories, no matter how small. Always keep your faith and know with God all things are possible.

This journey must begin and continue with much prayer. As we studied earlier in our lesson on prayer, God hears us when we pray anything according to His will and it is God's will for you to have a strong, healthy, and Christ-centered family. Prayer will be our best and most important resource for this journey.

God created the family in the garden, and it has always been the plan for humanity to have a family. The Scriptures have much to say about family and how we treat one another in each respective role. Below we will see what the Scriptures teach about the roles of each immediate family member.

Husband:

"Husbands, love your wives, even as Christ also loved the church, and gave Himself for it; That He might sanctify and cleanse it with the washing of water by the word, That He might present it to himself a glorious church, not having spot, or wrinkle, or any such thing; but that it should be holy and without blemish. So ought men to love their wives as their own bodies. He that loveth his wife loveth himself" (Eph 5:25-28 KJV).

"Husbands, love your wives, and be not bitter against them" (Col 3:19 KJV).

God commands husbands to love their wives as Christ loved the church and to love them as their own flesh. When men do not love their wife as they should, they are not fulfilling God's plan for the father of the family. If we love them as Christ loved the church and as ourselves, then we will love them even when they are not living in a way that pleases us. We will love them despite their weaknesses, shortcomings, and failures. We will always be merciful and take actions to help encourage and edify them to reach the full potential God has given them. You must show patience in every area and at all times. Your motives should always be to generate good and not be selfish about what you do and how you do it. Jesus gave His life for us while we were yet sinners, and we should have the same attitude toward our wives.

Just before these verses in Ephesians, God says to wives that they should submit. However, men loving their wives is not conditional on the wife submitting. He should love whether or not she submits. By doing this, we are saying that we trust God by our obedience to His word

88

and this releases God to work on our family. God honors our obedience to His word because it demonstrates our faith in Him. If we do not do as He teaches, we are saying with our actions we don't trust God.

Father:

"And, ye fathers, provoke not your children to wrath: but bring them up in the nurture and admonition of the Lord" (Eph 6:4 KJV).

"Fathers, provoke not your children to anger, lest they be discouraged" (Col 3:21 KJV).

A father is defined as a man who has begotten a child. This verse tells us that fathers are to bring up their children in the teachings of the Lord and to not "provoke them to wrath," or badger and shame them until they hate their father. Discipline and correction are most effective when done with love and patience. It is the father's responsibility to teach his children about God. This is done by teaching them His word but even more so by demonstrating it in the life we live and the example we set for them. It is the responsibility of the father to know God and to know the word of God and then live a life that models self-control and obedience to God and His word.

Wife:

"Wives, submit yourselves unto your own husbands, as unto the Lord. For the husband is the head of the wife, even as Christ is the head of the church: and He is the savior of the body" (Eph 5:22-23 KJV).
Wives are instructed to submit to their husbands. By submitting to their husbands, they are showing a proper relationship to authority. When they submit to and respect authority, it will help children understand their need to submit to the authority over them.
It demonstrates trust and faith in God and His word, which, in turn, releases God to work in our marriage. The Scripture gives us a very clear example of this.
"In the same way, you wives must accept the authority of your husbands. Then, even if some refuse to obey the Good News, your godly

lives will speak to them without any words. They will be won over by observing your pure and reverent lives" (1 Pt 3:1-2 NLT).

Mother:

"I will therefore that the younger women marry, bear children, guide the house, give none occasion to the adversary to speak reproachfully" (1 Tm 5:14 KJV).

"That they may teach the young women to be sober, to love their husbands, to love their children, To be discreet, chaste, keepers at home, good, obedient to their own husbands, that the word of God be not blasphemed" (Ti 2:4-5 KJV).

Mothers are instructed to bear children, love their husbands, guide the home, obey, submit, and teach their children. By doing so, their children will grow up being taught to honor God's word. To many in our society, these Scriptures are offensive and looked down upon even by people who confess to be Christians. No matter how conflicting these Scriptures may be with our society and culture, they are still the word of God and when obeyed will produce a strong, healthy, and Christ-centered family. God does not allow us to pick and choose which Scriptures we embrace and which ones we don't because they are all the inspired, infallible word of God and they work when applied.

Children:

"Honour thy father and thy mother: that thy days may be long upon the land which the LORD thy God giveth thee" (Ex 20:12 KJV).

"Children, obey your parents in the Lord: for this is right. Honour thy father and mother; which is the first commandment with promise; That it may be well with thee, and thou mayest live long on the earth" (Eph 6:1-3 KJV).

Children are to obey and honor their parents. This means that they are to obey in a respectful way that adds value to the whole family as well as their parents. God promises that those who honor their parents will live longer lives than they would if they were disobedient, hateful, and disrespectful to their mother and father. This commandment is not made null and void because our parents were not good parents. We should still honor them in obedience to God and because they gave us the opportunity of life and to become God's child and fulfill His purpose for our lives on the earth. When we honor God with our obedience to His word, He honors the promise He made.

Siblings:

"Rebuke not an elder, but intreat him as a father; and the younger men as brethren; The elder women as mothers; the younger as sisters, with all purity. Honour widows that are widows indeed" (1 Tm 5:1-3 KJV).

Now that we know what our roles and responsibilities are as family and how we are to love, honor, respect, and treat each family member, we can begin the healing journey. It is easy to pray and ask God to heal all the past and present hurts and problems, but without obedience to His word it will more than likely never happen. As we saw in the teaching, our obedience releases God to work in His way by His power, which is far better than anything we can do in an attempt to fix things and bring healing. God wants to heal and restore the family but often He cannot, or better yet, will not, because we are in the way with our own ideas and efforts of how to do what only God can do. Our obedience to God's word puts our trust and dependence in Him, and when our hope is in Him we will not be disappointed.

"And this hope will not lead to disappointment. For we know how dearly God loves us, because He has given us the Holy Spirit to fill our hearts with His love" (Rom 5:5 NLT).

To bring healing and restoration, someone has to decide to honor and obey God's word and be the godly family member who lives up to the responsibilities and roles as taught in the word of God.

We cannot allow the actions of another person, even a family member, to be the justification for our actions and behavior. We must live out God's word regardless of whether anyone else does or does not. We must also take into consideration the damage we have created with our past addictions. The trust and respect that we may have destroyed, the hurt and disappointments we may have caused, just to name a few damages we may have done. Although God has forgiven you and you are free from all the condemnation and guilt of these things, you must be patient and give God time to heal those you have hurt.

It is my experience that when a person has undergone a true change but the family is skeptical and guarded that it can cause discouragement and disappointment to the one who has experienced the change. You cannot allow this to happen. Understand that God, time, and your steadfast proof of the change God has made in your life will work in rebuilding trust and confidence in the relationships. Restoration can and does happen, but I have seen it takes time, patience, and steadfast obedience to God and His word.

# CHAPTER 17

## God in My Workplace (Work Ethics)

Addiction in most cases creates a lot of dysfunction in our lives that spills over into our job and job performance. Because we have financial responsibilities and obligations, our job or business, which is our source of income, can have a huge effect and influence on our lives. It can be a blessing, but it can also create a great deal of stress, which can lead to relapse and contribute to substance abuse so it becomes a key to living an addiction-free life.

In many cases, I have found that people had job and career issues prior to addiction and those problems were a contributing factor to their addiction because of self-medicating with drugs and alcohol to deal with the stress. In people where this was not the issue they, for the most part, developed problems in their jobs and it then became a contributing factor to their addiction. If it had not, it would only be a matter of time until it did.

As you progress in your journey with God and a life free from addiction, you will find that God desires for you to be blessed. He provides every opportunity for your needs to be met and for you to prosper in life. I do not believe prosperity is measured by the size of your house or the type of car you drive or even the kind of clothes you wear. I define prosperity as having my daily needs met, having enough money to save, and having money to give. I call it having seed to eat, seed to save, and seed to sow. God promises us that if we would seek first His Kingdom and righteousness, He would provide us with the provisions for life (Mt 6:25-33). This does not mean God will rain hundred-dollar bills from heaven, but it does mean He will provide the opportunity for you to work and provide.

I have seen God provide people with amazing opportunities through employment of business ventures but then watch as they lost it because of bad work ethics or job performance. Living godly and holy lives has as much to do with how we perform on our jobs as it does with abstaining from certain sins. The word of God has much to say about how we treat our employment and employers as well as how employers treat their business and employees. I want us to look at some Scriptures that are applicable to this subject.

"Slaves, obey your earthly masters in everything you do. Try to please them all the time, not just when they are watching you. Serve them sincerely because of your reverent fear of the Lord. Work willingly at whatever you do, as though you were working for the Lord rather than for people. Remember that the Lord will give you an inheritance as your reward, and that the Master you are serving is Christ. But if you do what is wrong, you will be paid back for the wrong you have done. For God has no favorites" (Col 3:22-25 NLT).

In this Scripture Paul addresses slaves, but this can very easily be applied to our culture as it relates to an employee working for an employer.

Paul says that we should obey our earthly masters (employers, bosses, supervisors, etc.). Insubordination and not following instructions is the number one cause to be dismissed from a job. Our responsibility as an employee is to do what we are told and please our employer, regardless of whether we like them or agree with them. They are in charge and have been given the authority and responsibility to have a task carried out, so therefore our responsibility is to please that boss or supervisor by doing what they ask with a good and positive attitude. Let me note that there may be special circumstances where we are asked to do something that violates our godly convictions but we will address that later. Paul says we should serve our master, employer, boss, supervisor, etc. in all that we do. He says we should try to please them all the time even when they are not watching us. This is called integrity. So many times people will slack on their duties or responsibility because no one is watching or they feel that they can get away with it. This is not integrity. It can also be the reason why you would be looked over for a promotion, advancement, or even a raise. People who just get by with doing as little as possible are the first ones to be laid off if there is a problem. Doing our best at all times and seeking to please our employer in all we do provides job security in most cases and also becomes the reason we are promoted, advanced, and given raises. You prove yourself to be an asset to that person or company that they value you and see you as indispensable.

The next instruction is to work willingly. This means that you carry out your responsibilities with a good and positive attitude showing eagerness, enthusiasm, and excellence. Many people do what they are asked but with a reluctant attitude that says, "I don't care," and they usually do a mediocre job. The task you may be asked to do may not be what you desire, but you remain obligated to do it with the same positive attitude. People who have a bad attitude about their job or employer/supervisor tend to create an unpleasant work environment for everyone, and all too often their negative attitude becomes contagious. This is not good for anyone, employee or employer.

The Scripture goes on to instruct us to work at our job as if we were working for the Lord. No one should want to do a mediocre job for the Lord or do it with a bad, reluctant attitude. Everything we do for the Lord should be done with excellency and with a positive, willing attitude. Many times, our attitude and job performance are determined by how our employer/supervisor treats us, but this should not be the case. We are told in the Scripture that we are not to return evil for evil but to overcome evil with good (Rom 12:17-21 NLT), and this should be the case as it relates to our job. If we do our job as unto the Lord and not to men, then we will always do it to the very best of our ability and with a positive attitude and from a heart of servitude.

Many times we determine our job performance and attitude based on how much money we make, but that should never be the case with us as Christians. God's word promises He will provide us with an inheritance because when we do our job as to Him then He is the one that will reward us. God has ways to bless you and promote you that go beyond your job or employer so never limit what God can do. Never allow how much money you are paid to determine your job performance and attitude so that God can reward you with the inheritance He can provide. I assure you it will be more than any company, business, or person could pay you.

The Scripture closes this word with a very stern warning. If we do what is wrong, we will be paid back for that wrong we did because God has no favorites. Just because we are a Christian and have been given a new life does not exclude us from our responsibilities as an employee and from doing what His word teaches us.

There may be situations that arise where you are employed by a company that does not operate ethically and may ask you to do things that go against your godly convictions. In this case, you conduct yourself in a godly manner and resign from that job in a respectful and ethical way. Be honest, respectful, and kind when you leave and God will surely provide a new and better job for you.

If you are a Christian employer or business owner, your responsibilities and obligations are just as important as your employees'. The Scripture has much to say about your responsibility.

"Masters, be just and fair to your slaves. Remember that you also have a Master—in heaven" (Col 4:1 NLT).

An employer or a supervisor should always treat employees justly and fairly. This means that you treat them with respect and honor their good works. You should reward them fairly for the work they provide. Look out for them, and do what is right for them and not just what is right for the business or profits. A business is simply a business, and your employees are people our heavenly Father cares for. Your example in how you treat them and communicate with them reveals Christ to them. The greatest sermon we preach is not with the words we speak but with the example we set. Always remember you have a heavenly Master watching over you at all times. Treat your employees in a way that pleases God.

# CHAPTER 18

## Money Management

Finances can create more stress in our life than most any other thing that we deal with on a day-to-day basis. It can be the cause of relationship problems and many other things because stress can be a trigger to cause a person to self-medicate or to relapse. Therefore, money management is a matter that must be addressed, making it key to living a life free of addiction.

In his day, John D. Rockefeller was one of the richest men in the world. For all practical purposes, his money was virtually limitless. Once, an interviewer asked him, "How much money is enough?" Rockefeller replied, "Just a little bit more!"

As outrageous as it sounds, haven't we all been there? Whatever our income level, we think to ourselves, *If only I had just a little bit more...* Then, at last, our budget would have some breathing room and we will be satisfied with our finances.

But Rockefeller's response pokes a hole in that theory. The truth is, control over money has less to do with how much we make, and a lot more to do with how we manage what we have. Financial health is important not only to our bank balance but to the atmosphere in our home. More marriages have blown apart over financial issues than almost any other factor.

We need to recognize that managing money is a spiritual issue. Did you know that Jesus spoke more about money than He did about any other topic? In fact, 15 percent of all the recorded words of Jesus are on the subject of money—more than His teachings on heaven and hell combined.

Why did money matter so much to Jesus?

To Jesus, our attitude toward money is crucial because it is a reflection of our attitude toward God. As Larry Burkett said, "You can tell more about the spiritual lives of a couple by looking at their checkbook than by anything else."

Everything we have comes from God. He owns it, and He entrusts it to us to use for His purposes. True financial success does not come from accumulating a large surplus in our bank account, but from following God's plan for our finances. As we do this, He will provide for all of our needs.

Money problems can become a trigger for a person to resort back to old addictions to self-medicate. Do money problems cause tension and stress in your life? Do you find it difficult to manage your finances and to know where you really stand? If so, these three simple steps may help you successfully manage your finances.

1. Give to God first.

As Christians, our first priority should be obeying God and His word as it relates to our money. God and His word should always come first. The issue of managing all of our gifts, including our finances, is of great importance to God. Figuring out how much to give as a minimum is fairly easy, as the Bible instructs us to give a tithe, or one-tenth of our income back to God. This is a great starting point for Christian giving.

You may ask the question, "How can I possibly do this when I am already struggling to get by?" You may be thinking, *How is this going to make things better and not make it worse?* The truth is there will never be "enough" to give. If we wait until all of our needs and desires are met before we start to give, it will never happen. Statistics show that the more a person makes, the less they are likely to give, percentage-wise. The more we have, the more we think we need.

People today talk very little about their actual salary or how much they are worth. Like all secrets, this gives far more power to money than it actually deserves. Similarly, and more properly, people who tithe do not go around boasting about it. But I would like to challenge you to ask people you trust whether or not they tithe. If they do tithe, ask them about their experience. In all my discussions with people about money I have never heard anyone say that their financial problems started or got worse once they started to tithe. On the contrary, people who tithe seem to be better off than those who don't. It is one of the many mysteries of how God works.

2. Set aside funds for regular savings.

It is important to establish the discipline required to save money for unforeseen expenses and large purchases, such as the down payment for a home, college education, vacations, and retirement. This will allow you to spend from cash resources and eliminate the need to borrow money when it is not necessary. You will be surprised by how much you can accumulate by a simple but disciplined savings program.

Do not plan your savings after you plan your spending because experience shows that those who try this rarely succeed. You may decide to make this a percentage of your income, and this will probably change as you go through the various stages of life. All financial planners will tell you that the sooner you start saving the more you will be able to save, so plan to start right now.

The issue of savings is one that requires a balanced perspective. The Bible makes it clear that we are supposed to save, but it never tells us how much is too much or too little. The purpose of saving is to provide for legitimate future needs, and for some it will allow you to become one of those special people who can fund important needs of others.

3. Spend the rest on what you need.

The key to good money management is expense management. We need to learn to live below our means and be content with what God has given us. This is hard for all of us, but it is an important life lesson. The key is to develop a good budget, which is basically a spending plan. Invest the time in learning to use helpful tools, such as a computer spreadsheet or a financial program. If you have never had a budget, spend two or three months tracking your spending. Try keeping a log every time you spend money so that you can improve your budget understanding. Then examine your habits and determine how you would like to proceed and where you need to cut back.

Be committed to this plan and do not be discouraged if you do not see results for the first two or three months. It takes time to break old habits, and if you have gotten yourself into a financial hole it will take time to dig back out. Be patient and stick to your budget spending because it really does work.

Finally, two more important points to consider:

1.  Always discuss finances as a couple if you are married. One spouse likely has more financial skills than the other and will naturally take the lead, but this is no excuse for the other spouse not to be involved in the family financial situation. You both need to understand the issues that you are facing, and make decisions as a team. Financial problems are listed as a major cause of strife in the marriage relationship, and it often starts when one partner is being kept in the dark.

2.  If you have financial problems, seek help before it is too late. Financial problems can be solved, but it often means changes, some of which may not be that easy. A qualified financial planner can help you identify the problem areas and think through solutions that will work for your family. If you cannot afford a professional financial planner, you can usually find someone in your church that can help you voluntarily. Make sure that the person you seek to help you has a proven track record of managing money; secondly make sure they can be trusted with the confidentiality of your personal business.

Above all, listen to what God may be saying to you through your financial circumstances. Finances can be a dividing factor in marriage, but they can also bring you together in a new and deeper way, as you trust God together and follow His plan.

If you are willing to follow this simple plan and begin to intelligently and prayerfully give away 10 percent of your income, I believe your financial situation will improve. More importantly, you will be storing up treasures in heaven, which is what really counts.

# CHAPTER 19

## Time Management

Time management can be a result of a self-disciplined life, but it can also be an asset in developing a self-disciplined life. Self-discipline and time management are critical for recovery, so therefore they are key to living an addiction-free life.

If you once lived a disciplined life and managed your time well, there is a good chance you no longer possess those traits due to your past addiction. There are certainly exceptions to the rule, but odds are you need to implement more discipline in your life and time management will help you accomplish that goal.

To discipline your life, you must first understand the value of time because it is the one thing you cannot create more of, or purchase. All you can do is manage the time that you have so it is most effectively used. Knowing that we only get a certain amount of time helps us to place the proper value on time and what we value we will take care of and pay attention to. We are given 24 hours in a day with approximately 12 hours of daytime to accomplish tasks so our time is limited so to speak. God shows us another way of understanding the limit of time that should certainly raise the value of time in your eyes.

"LORD, remind me how brief my time on earth will be.
    Remind me that my days are numbered—
    how fleeting my life is.
You have made my life no longer than the width of my hand.
    My entire lifetime is just a moment to you;
    at best, each of us is but a breath." *Interlude*
"We are merely moving shadows,
    and all our busy rushing ends in nothing.
We heap up wealth,
    not knowing who will spend it.
And so, Lord, where do I put my hope?
    My only hope is in you.

Rescue me from my rebellion.
>> Do not let fools mock me." (Ps 39:4-8 NLT)

The psalmist asked the Lord for something very significant—remind me how brief my time on earth will be.

When we really comprehend what short amount of time we have, time becomes very valuable and our need to use it wisely becomes a priority. The psalmist adds in Psalm 90:10 that the average lifespan of a person is 70 to 80 years and that lines up with the statistics of the average lifespan of a human. This is certainly not guaranteeing how long an individual will live because our days are in God's hands according to other Scriptures, but it does cause us to think of how short our time is.

Recently I drew out a timeline from 0 years to 70 years in 10-year increments. I then marked my age, which is 50, and realized just how short my time is to accomplish and fulfill what God has created me for. It is a good exercise to get a real grasp on how valuable time is.

I remember when I was 20 thinking 50 was old, but now that I am 50, I realize how quickly I went from 20 to 50. I sometimes ask myself where did the years go and how did they pass by so quickly. It is time to start managing your time and using it wisely. We have looked at the motivation to manage our time, now let's look at how.

1. Prioritize, organize, and set goals.
   "This is not good!" Moses' father-in-law exclaimed. "You're going to wear yourself out—and the people, too. This job is too heavy a burden for you to handle all by yourself. Now listen to me, and let me give you a word of advice, and may God be with you. You should continue to be the people's representative before God, bringing their disputes to him. Teach them God's decrees, and give them His instructions. Show them how to conduct their lives. But select from all the people some capable, honest men who fear God and hate bribes. Appoint them as leaders over groups of one thousand, one hundred, fifty, and ten. (Ex 18:17-21 NLT)

2. Put God first. This is critical. If you don't have your relationship with God in order, then how can you expect to know what the right thing is you are supposed to be doing? Spend time daily in God's word and in

prayer. Ask the Lord to give you wisdom in setting your priorities for the day. Your goals for today also hinge on future plans that God has for you. Allow Him to lead you through His revealed will in the Bible. This means that your first priority is to always obey God's word. However, there are many decisions that you must make that God does not give clear guidance to in the Bible. From there, allow His Spirit to lead you.

3. Know God's will. If you don't know what God has designed you to do, then it is hard to know what your ultimate priorities should be. Seek to know God's will for your life. Sometimes, people talk about God's will like it is something God has hidden from you. This is not the case. God wants you to know what His will is.

Primarily, it starts with obeying God's word every day. When you obey the principles set out in the Bible, then you will be sensitive to the Holy Spirit's leading so that you can know and obey God's plan.

Time management really does not matter if you are not focusing your time on the right things.

4. Find the right priorities. There is a lot of talk among ministers as to what your priority structure should be. Should it be: family first and church second? Or, church first and family second? I believe if you put God first, then you will know what should be second and third on the list. Allow the Holy Spirit to guide your decisions, and you will sometimes make the choice to put family over church ministry and sometimes church ministry over family.

Of course, you may not be a minister, but this principle still applies. Put God first and allow the Holy Spirit to help you know what your priorities in any situation should be.

5. Take time to think and plan. This is a time to sit down and think about what has been accomplished over the last week and what is coming up in the next week or months. This doesn't have to take too much time, but it needs to be done. If you don't think through your upcoming events, then you won't know how each piece fits together in the bigger picture of your life.

I recently spoke with a builder who said that he usually accomplishes more on a job the days he works by himself than on the days he works with a crew. He knew that on days he was by himself he was forced to think through the job. He had to plan and make conscientious decisions based on what a one-man crew could do. But on days he worked with other people, he spent less time thinking because he assumed that anything that came up he could tackle. The truth is that thinking is what makes the difference on being able to get things done.

6. Do important tasks, not just urgent ones. We so often get wrapped up in doing urgent things and not important ones. This does not mean you shouldn't take care of the urgent matters that come up, but don't let them derail you. Sometimes urgent items are important, but many times they are not.

Often an urgent matter is caused because someone else did not take care of the important tasks in their own workflow. This may be a time to educate them and allow them to fail in an area. If you will not respect your own priorities and tasks, you can't expect others to respect them for you.

7. Write things down. Have a way to capture ideas that come to you. If you don't capture and remember what it is you want to accomplish, there is no way to guarantee you will do them. There are many smartphone apps that can help you with that, as well as voice recorders.
You should choose a tool that you will always have with you and that is quick and easy enough to encourage you to capture your thoughts. For many people this is a pen and piece of paper.

8. Know what needs to be done. I love when I am talking with someone and I feel like I have the other's complete attention. It makes me feel important, and it elevates my respect for that person. To be the person who can devote your attention to others at the moment, you must know what needs to be done and what can be put off during that time. If you don't know what is on your calendar or your to-do list, then you cannot devote your attention to the task or person at hand.

9. Live as if today were your last. The Bible says we aren't given any promise of tomorrow (Prv 27:1 NLT). You need to live so that you accomplish what you believe is important at the moment based on your priorities and God's will at this time (Jas 4:14 NLT). This may be playing a board game with your children, preparing a sermon, or

fixing a leaky faucet. I can't tell you what is important, but you should know what that is. If you aren't sure, then you need to spend time with the other tips here.

10. Plan for tomorrow. While we should live knowing that tomorrow may never come, we also know that it is wise to plan for the future. Proverbs 6:6-8 (NLT) says we should take a lesson from the ant that plans for the future. Proverbs 16:9 (NLT) says that we should plan and allow God to direct us in and through our planning. If you don't sit down and count the cost of a project, there is no reasonable way to expect that it will be accomplished. Planning is necessary.

While you must plan, you should also be flexible in those plans and allow the Holy Spirit to guide you (Prv 16:9; 2 Cor 5:7 NLT).